Science and the Human Imagination:
Albert Einstein

THE LEVERTON LECTURE SERIES

THE LEVERTON LECTURE SERIES 5

Science and the Human Imagination: Albert Einstein

Papers and Discussions by
Jeremy Bernstein *and* Gerald Feinberg

Including Two Lectures on New Jersey's
Contributions to the Chemical Industry and
Chemical Education

Papers and Discussions by
Henry B. Hass *and* A. K. Bose

Edited by Charles Angoff

Rutherford • Madison • Teaneck
Fairleigh Dickinson University Press
London: Associated University Presses

Physics

QC

16

E 5

B 46

Associated University Presses, Inc.
Cranbury, New Jersey 08512

Associated University Presses
Magdalen House
136–148 Tooley Street
London SE1 2TT, England

Library of Congress Cataloging in Publication Data

Bernstein, Jeremy, 1924–
    Science and the human imagination.

    (The Leverton lecture series ; 5)
    1. Einstein, Albert, 1879–1955—Addresses, essays, lectures.
2. Physicists—United States—Biography—Addresses, essays, lectures.
3. Physics—History—Addresses, essays, lectures. 4. Chemical
engineering—New Jersey—History—Addresses, essays, lectures.
5. Chemistry—Study and teaching—New Jersey—Addresses, essays,
lectures. I. Feinberg, Gerald, 1933–   joint author. II. Hass,
Henry Bohn, 1902–   New Jersey's contributions to the
chemical industry and chemical education. 1978. III. Title.
IV. Series: Leverton lecture series ; 5.
QC16.E5B46   530'.092'4   [B]   77-92565
ISBN 0-8386-2223-2

Contents

5

Foreword

In this latest addition to the publications in the Leverton Lecture Series two major topics of broad national, and indeed, international interest are discussed by world-renowned authorities. The topics are "Science and the Human Imagination: Albert Einstein" and "New Jersey's Contributions to the Chemical Industry and Chemical Education." The four lecturers are fully identified in the introductory remarks to their talks. After each series of lectures there was a short period of questions, answers, and amplifications. This part of the program (along with a good deal of the lectures proper) was first taped, then transcribed. All who have dealt with the problem of transcribing tapes know the difficulties involved. Occasionally the tape will fade out as the lecturer moves around, and sometimes, when a member of the audience asks a question, he will forget to give his name. There are other troublesome matters. This is why in the discussions questions and answers are sometimes introduced with the simple Q and A. Further identification would, of course, be preferable, but the content of both questions and answers is there, and that, after all, is what is more important.

The two sets of lectures in the present volume are part of a four-year project instituted at the Rutherford Campus of Fairleigh Dickinson University to highlight the contributions of New Jersey to the national culture, on the occasion of the celebration of the bicentennial of the founding of the Republic.

Charles Angoff
Professor Emeritus
of English, Fairleigh
Dickinson University

7

DR. MORRIS LEVERTON

Financier Morris Leverton, sponsor of the lecture series, has been a member of the Board of Overseers at Fairleigh Dickinson and a member of the President's Council at the University.

He currently serves as the University's Board of Overseers' representative to Wroxton College, FDU's campus in England.

Dr. Leverton's interest in Fairleigh Dickinson University is one of his foremost and ongoing concerns.

The Program

Introductory Speakers

Dr. Saul K. Fenster

Dr. Charles Angoff

Dr. Harvey H. Bird

Main Speakers

Dr. Jeremy Bernstein

Dr. Gerald Feinberg

Topic

Science and the Human Imagination:
Albert Einstein

The Participants

DR. JEREMY BERNSTEIN is Professor of Physics at Stevens Institute of Technology. He received his Ph.D. from Harvard University, and has been a member of the Institute for Advanced Study in Princeton. He is the author of numerous technical papers, and six books, including *Einstein*, which was nominated for a National Book award in 1974.

DR. GERALD FEINBERG is Professor of Physics at Columbia University. He received his Ph.D. from Columbia University, and has been a member of the Institute for Advanced Study in Princeton. He is the author of many professional and popular articles on physics and philosophy, and a major work: *The Prometheus Project—Mankind's Search for Long-range Goals.*

DR. SAUL K. FENSTER is Professor of Mechanical Engineering and Provost of the Rutherford Campus of Fairleigh Dickinson University.

DR. CHARLES ANGOFF is Professor Emeritus of English at the Rutherford Campus of Fairleigh Dickinson University and is the Leverton Lecture Series Chairman.

DR. HARVEY H. BIRD is Associate Professor of Physics at the Rutherford Campus of Fairleigh Dickinson University and is the coordinator of this evening's program.

Science
and the
Human Imagination:
Albert Einstein

Science and the Human Imagination: Albert Einstein

A. Jeremy Bernstein

DR. ANGOFF: I feel wonderful that we are so crowded on an occasion such as this. Nobody is running for office. A couple of distinguished people are going to tell us about important things, really important things. But all this was made possible by two wonderful people who have been enormously generous to Fairleigh Dickinson University and are directly responsible for the Leverton Lecture Series. I would like to have them stand up. Dr. and Mrs. Morris Leverton.

Welcome to another of the Leverton Lecture Series on the Rutherford Campus. There are three major Leverton Lecture Series at Fairleigh Dickinson University, one at each of the three campuses. The one at Rutherford has been devoted, during the past three years, to an examination of New Jersey's contribution to the national culture on various levels of intellectual and creative activities. Thus we have dealt with poetry, chiefly in the person of the pediatrician-poet Dr. William Carlos Williams, who graced Rutherford with his presence for the greater part of his mature creative years. He was a sort of patron saint of Fairleigh Dickinson University, and incidentally, as I can testify from personal

13

knowledge gathered in my travels abroad, Dr. Williams is the American poet now read by more Europeans than any other American poet, and most respected by the most knowledgeable critics.

The second in the Leverton Lecture Series at Rutherford dealt with no less a man than Jonathan Edwards, first president of what later became Princeton University, a theologian of transcendent importance in American history, and a philosopher of such depth and breadth that some cognoscenti have not hesitated to call him the American Immanuel Kant.

There was also a program on New Jersey's contribution to the research into the effect of environment on our well-being. Three eminent ecologists enlightened us on this topic. There were also programs concerned with painting and music and other areas of cultural enrichment. Only last spring we had an exciting program about the first governor of New Jersey, William Livingston, whose ideas had a great influence on the evolution of American law.

Several of these lectures have appeared in book form under the rubrics of Leverton Lecture Series 1, 2, and so on. Judging by the reviews in the learned journals, it is clear that the Leverton Lecture volumes have joined the stream of enduring scholarship.

This evening, as you can see from your programs, two eminent authorities will talk on "Science and the Human Imagination: Einstein." I like that title. What comes after the colon summarizes what goes before. Einstein was a scientist who played the violin and had a special love for the music of Wolfgang Amadeus Mozart, a human angel if there ever was one. This to me means that Einstein had the heart of a poet; which also means that he was moved by the evidence of things not seen and was looking for the substance of things hoped for—in short, a man of imagination, the essential quality of every scientist as well as artist. No less a philosopher than John Dewey, in *The Quest for Certainty*, has said, "Every great advance in science has issued from a new audacity of the imagination." But enough of my philosophical meanderings. You will soon hear from two men who really know what science is, and how it's related to the human imagination. Dr. Harvey Bird, Associate Professor of Physics at Fairleigh Dickinson University, who is chiefly responsible for getting our two experts into this lecture hall, will now introduce them.

DR. BIRD: Thank you, Dr. Angoff. One of the most important words in the theme for this evening's program is the word *human,* and I would like to make the following observations about that word. All deep and creative insight into nature results only from man's entering into his most open and his most receptive mode of being. That is when he is most at one with himself and his world, in other words, when he is his most human. That is the only way that he can see the incredible harmony and unity that underlie all of nature, and this is true whether he is a scientist or a philosopher, an artist or a poet. It was certainly true for Albert Einstein, who was a deeply human person and one of the profoundest thinkers of all time. With his deep and penetrating insight into nature, he radically transformed our concepts of the world in which we live, and laid the foundations for most of twentieth-century science.

This evening we are indeed fortunate to have with us two outstanding scientists who will tell us more about this man: his life, his creative work, his impact upon our twentieth-century life and thought. These two gentlemen are well known to each other; they work together, and they have worked together on this evening's program; and in order not to interrupt the continuity of the evening. I would like to introduce both of them to you at this time.

Our first speaker will be Dr. Jeremy Bernstein. Dr. Bernstein received his Ph.D. from Harvard University, was a member of the Institute for Advanced Study in Princeton, and is now Professor of Physics at Stevens Institute of Technology in Hoboken. He has been a visiting professor at many universities and institutions around the world, among which are Oxford, the University of Islamabad, Rockefeller University, Ecole Polytechnic, and Cern. He is a staff member of the *New Yorker*, and is the author of fifty technical papers and six books on a wide variety of topics including *Ascent: A History of Climbing; A Profile of Nepal; Elementary Particles and their Currents*; and a recent book entitled *Einstein*, which was nominated for the National Book Award in 1974.

Professor Bernstein will be followed on our program this evening by Dr. Gerald Feinberg. Dr. Feinberg received his Ph.D. from Columbia University, was a member of the Institute for Advanced Study in Princeton, and is now Professor of Physics at Columbia. He has been an Overseas Fellow at Churchill College in Cambridge and a visiting professor at Rockefeller University. He has been a consultant with the Stanford Linear Accelerator Center and with *Scientific American*, and is currently a consultant with the Brookhaven National Laboratory. His honors include fellowships from the National Science Foundation, the Alfred P. Sloan Foundation, and the Guggenheim Foundation. He is the author of many professional and technical and popular articles on physics and philosophy, including a major work entitled "The Prometheus Project; Mankind's Search for Long-range Goals."

Now I would like to request that the audience withhold the asking of their questions until after both speakers have spoken, and we will conclude the evening with a question-and-answer period. I will now turn the program over to our two speakers. We will first hear from Professor Bernstein.

DR. BERNSTEIN: Thank you very much. It is a great pleasure to be here. It's also unusual, I think, to be able to speak in front of a living donor. Usually these are memorial lectures and the donor is unable to criticize. If we give bad lectures, the donor can give us the works. The subject is so vast that Gerry Feinberg and I have decided that we would split it up into two parts and each of us will speak for something like forty minutes. If I go on beyond forty minutes, Feinberg will give me a hook and I will disappear up the ceiling. We will divide up the subject in something like the following way: I will talk about Einstein through 1905 and the invention of the special theory of relativity. Feinberg will discuss Einstein's contributions to the quantum theory, which means the period 1905 and thereafter. Such is the magnitude of the scientific creativity of the man that probably neither of us will have time, unless asked in the question period, to discuss the general theory of relativity, gravitation, and cosmology, about which one could have several evenings just like this, with many speakers. The magnitude of the man's creativity is really beyond explanation.

Now, I would like to make the following additional general remark: It is true, I think, that Einstein was a humanist in some sense, and very much concerned with the human race as a whole. On the other hand, people who knew him, among which number I am not, describe, characteristically, that when he was approached as a person, he seemed to retreat into a kind of shell. In other words, he presented a rather fascinating but elusive personality, and he was probably less interested in the individual affairs of individual people than he was in the larger concerns of mankind as a whole. In some of his writing, he speaks or writes in a tone of—I don't know whether the proper term is *contempt for,* or *indifference to*, the merely personal. In other words, the concerns that were merely the concerns of *a* person, personal concerns, he seemed to regard as somewhat trivial. He spoke sometimes with a certain regret of having a stomach, things of that kind, so we would, I think, be doing this lecture series and Einstein himself a disservice if we devoted our lectures simply to the "merely personal"—that is, simply telling you stories about how he was, or was not, charming about this, that, and the other thing. I don't think we would be doing a service to the subject if we did that. So I want to divide my remarks into four parts.

The first part I want to discuss is the state of physics in the nineteenth century as it confronted Einstein. In the second part of the talk, having said I wouldn't, I want to talk a little about the merely personal and describe something of the circumstances of Einstein's early life, especially since I think it does reflect upon the way in which his creativity manifested itself. Third, I want to talk about how Eintsein confronted the problems of nineteenth-century physics as he found them, and last, if there is any time, I want to talk about the reception that the special theory of relativity received after its creation.

So first, as to the status of nineteenth-century physics: nineteenth-century physics had two great themes; on the one hand, there was the mechanics of Newton, invented in the seventeenth century. The principal idea of this was that acceleration, or changes in motion, was produced by forces. That was the principal theme of Newton's mechanics; and by postulating certain forces he was able to derive practically everything about the motion of objects. In particular, he was able to predict the motions of the moon and the solar system. Now, working underneath this enormously successful scheme were some rather obscure philosophical and theological hypotheses. In particular, it was crucial for Newton to be able to say what an acceleration was, since in his scheme of things it was the forces that produced acceleration. Since he was a theologically oriented man, it was satisfactory to him for some motions to be able to say that the absolute determination of them resided in the sensorium of God. He frequently resorted to theological images when challenged on points in his physics, some of which turned out on later examination to be rather obscure. What happened over the subsequent two hundred years was that these theological underpinnings of Newtonian mechanics were forgotten or ignored because of the great practical success of the theory. Nobody bothered to look the gift horse in the mouth. There was this marvelous theory, and the fact that there were some obscure points here and there didn't bother anybody especially. Thus one of the great themes of nineteenth-century physics was the enormous practical success of Newtonian mechanics.

Then there was a subject that was really peculiar to the nineteenth century: the theory, the unified theory, of electricity and magnetism. Magnetism was something that had been known as a sort of curiosity since the ancient Greeks, and electricity, in one form or another, had been known for a long time; Benjamin Franklin made the first serious electrical theory with moving positive and negative charges; but that electricity and magnetism were part of a unity was really a product of the nineteenth century. It finally culminated in the invention by James Clark Maxwell of the equations that bear his name, which describe electricity and magnetism. So, by the end of the nineteenth century, there were two structures, Newtonian mechanics and Maxwell's Theory, both of which appear to have great certitude, great power of prediction, but which very rapidly came into growing contradiction with each other. That was in some sense the drama of nineteenth-century physics: these two accepted theories appeared to be mutually contradictory. The contradiction manifested itself roughly in the following way: in the formulation of his theory, Maxwell had made use of a concept called the "luminiferous ether." As he viewed the propagation of electrical waves, it was rather like the propagation of sound; namely, when sound propagates, one can trace its propagation as the motion of a disturbance in a medium. Maxwell and other nineteenth-century physicists envisioned the propagation of light, which Maxwell had identified as an electromagnetic wave, in a similar way. A disturbance in the ether produced the wave, they said, and the light wave propagated along through the ether. The analogy between the propagation of light and the propagation of sound seemed to them very plausible. Now, you can always catch up with a sound wave; that is what *supersonic* means. You can move as fast as a sound wave. According to Newtonian mechanics, there was no reason to believe that one could not also catch up with a light wave. Newtonian mechanics said that one could attain *any* velocity if one were accelerated long enough. One could finally attain a velocity comparable to that of light and, at that velocity it turns out that the manifestation of the light would essentially disappear. There would no longer be a light wave. This seemed, particularly to the young Einstein, to be a very peculiar thing. In addition the question arose as to whether one could detect the motion of the earth through this hypothetical ether in which the light was being propagated. A very ingenious experiment was done by the American physicists Michelson and Morley to attempt to measure the motion of the earth through the ether. Maxwell himself had proposed this experiment. This motion should have been clearly detectable in the experiment of Michelson and Morley performed in 1887. Lo and behold, they found nothing! This was difficult for classical physics. To deal with it the great Dutch physicist Lorentz proposed a hypothesis that moving objects contracted in the direction of their motion. This was known as the Lorentz contraction hypothesis, and in an ad hoc sense, the Lorentz contraction hypothesis resolved the contradiction of the Michelson-Morley experiment but only by introducing this very strange idea—that matter contracts in the direction along which it is moving—a very, very peculiar idea, that Lorentz himself was not terribly pleased with as a fundamental theory. These then are a few themes that were in the nineteenth-century physics.

Now let me say a few words about the young Einstein. Einstein was born in 1879, which was coincidentally the year of the death of Maxwell. He was apparently not, as least so people said, an especially bright child. He seemed to be rather slow, and he didn't speak until rather late. His nurse referred to him as "father bore." He was, it appears, a somewhat verbally limited child. He was rather dreamy. He was preoccupied, it appears, with the construction of extremely elaborate card houses and things like that. He did not, apparently, show the kind of mathematical precocity that you really see in young mathematical prodigies, but I think nonetheless that he must have been pretty smart. He was attracted to science very early. In his autobiography, or what passes for his autobiography, which he wrote late in life (at age 67)—he referred to it as his "obituary" while writing it—he describes a little bit of the wonder that science produced in him as a child. He writes: "A wonder of such nature I experienced as a child of four or five years when my father showed me a compass. That this needle behaved in such a determined way, did not at all fit into the nature of events, which could find a place in the unconscious world of concepts: effect connected with direct touch. I can still remember, or I believe I can remember, that this experience made a deep and lasting impression on me. Something deeply hidden had to be behind things. What man sees before him from infancy causes no reaction of this kind. He is not surprised over the falling of bodies, concerning wind and rain, or concerning the moon, or about the fact that the moon does not fall down. Nor concerning the differences between living and nonliving matter." Einstein was, by the way, as he tells us in the "obituary," as a very young man a rather fanatical theologian, much to the dismay of his parents, who were not especially practicing Jews, certainly not orthodox. But young Einstein went to a Catholic gymnasium. He was born in Ulm and moved to Munich, went to a Catholic gymnasium there, and found the religious training of his early life very interesting. He apparently engaged in tremendous arguments with his family. He writes how it happened that he lost religion. He was given some popular science books, about which he writes: "Through the reading of popular science books, I soon reached a conviction that much in the stories of the Bible could not be true. The consequence was a positive orgy of free thinking, coupled with the impression that youth is potentially being deceived by the state through lies. It was a crushing impression. Suspicion against every kind of authority grew out of this experience. A skeptical attitude towards convictions which were alive in any specific social environment, an attitude which has never again left me, even though later on, because of a better insight into the causal connections it lost some of its original poignancy." He discovered geometry very young. This passage from his "obituary" convinces me that he was very unusual at that age, although he frequently made light of his mathematical abilities as a child. Nonetheless, he writes:

At the age of 12 I experienced a second wonder of a totally different nature [from the compass] in a lttle book, dealing with Euclidian plane geometry, which came into my hands at the beginning of the school year. Here were assertions as for example, intersections of the three altitudes of a triangle at one point, which were by no means evident, but nevertheless could be proved with such certainty that any doubt appeared to be out of the question.

This lucidity of certainty made an indescribable impression upon him.

That the axiom had to be accepted unproved did not disturb me. In any case, it was quite sufficient for me if I could peg proofs upon propositions, the validity of which did not seem to me to be dubious. For example, I remember that an uncle told me about the Pythagorean theorem before the holy geometry booklet had come into my hands. After much effort, I succeeded in proving this theorem on the basis of similarity of triangles. In doing so, it seemed to me evident that the relation of the size of the right handed right angle triangles would have to be completely determined by one of the acute angles. Only something which did not in a similar fashion seem to be evident, appears to me to be in need of any proof at all.

Well, I think that a child of twelve who discovers some of the basic results of Euclidian geometry is probably pretty well endowed mathematically. When Albert was about sixteen his father's family business failed. His father was in a kind of chemical electroplating business and appeared to be in a constant state of business failure, so the family kept moving from place to place. This time the family moved out of Germany to Italy. Einstein was left behind, in a gymnasium that he hated, and he devised a scheme to escape. He got a letter from a doctor asserting that his mental health would be imperiled if he had to remain in the gymnasium, but before he could present this letter, he was kicked out anyway. The teacher told him that his presence and his skeptical attitude were disturbing other students. At any rate he was thrown out, so this letter was not necessary. He returned to his family, in Italy, and there he engaged in a self-study program of mathematics and physics. He presented himself to the Technichse Hochschule in Zurich for entry at about age sixteen. He *failed* the entrance examination. He failed the parts of the examination dealing with languages and the like, although he impressed the director very favorably with his grasp of physics and mathematics. And so he spent a year in preparatory school in Arrau, in Switzerland. It was probably during this year, at age sixteen and seventeen, that his life really changed, because in this school, which was a rather progressive school, he was allowed the opportunity of doing experimentation, and given a good deal of time for thinking. It is very likely that during this year he really developed the taste and aptitude for scientific work. He then entered the technical Hochschule in Zurich, apparently a rather interesting place in those days. There were a lot of liberal currents floating around in Zurich. Tom Stoppaud, in his play *Travesties,* describes the Zurich of the First War somewhat later, noting that at this time there were Lenin, James Joyce, and Tristan Zara (who founded Dadaism), all living and working in Zurich. It was a very lively, almost revolutionary kind of place. One of the things it offered was the possibility for women to study in branches of science and engineering. Einstein, in fact, met his first wife in just that way. She was a student of science and engineering, and had come from Eastern Europe to study in Zurich because it was one of the few places, if not the only place on the European continent where women could study physics and engineering. Because of her, he very rarely went to classes. She went to classes and he studied her notes. He made a very unfavorable impression on his teachers. When Minkowski, who later became very important in the mathematical development of the theory of relativity, found out that it was Einstein who had created the theory, he was extremely shocked. He had been one of Einstein's teachers and had never expected anything good from "that lazy dog." Indeed, when Einstein left the Technichse Hochschule in 1901, he was not able to get a proper academic job, nor was he able to get any real job at all. Eventually, through the influence of the father of a classmate, he was able to secure a position as a patent examiner in the Swiss Patent Office in Berne. It is somewhat unclear how serious a job that was. Some people say that it was not a serious one, that it was a sinecure. I don't think so. From what I've been able to gather, I think it was a serious job. I think he spent eight hours a day examining patent applications and writing, in a very serious way, scientific and technical opinions of them. He was also the head of a growing family, with two sons. Furthermore, he had very little access to good library facilities. The library at the University at Berne was not very good; the library in physics in the patent office was apparently nonexistent. Despite all this, his first great creative period, from 1901 to 1905, occurred when Einstein was in the patent office in Berne, a job he dd not escape from until 1907–8. This partly explains, I think, the style of his first paper on the theory of relativity, written in 1905.

As I tried to indicate earlier, there were a great many ideas circulating among his contemporaries. Lorentz was writing about his contracting matter. The French mathematician Poincaré had some fairly vague ideas about the change in the measure of time as one goes from a moving to a resting system. But most of this was unknown to Einstein because he simply was not in the mainstream where the literature would have been available to him. He simply could not read the literature. He probably did not know about the Michelson experiment, mentioned earlier, which showed the undetectability of the motion of the earth through the ether. So in some sense his paper of 1905 on the special theory of relativity was almost a purely mental creation, without the sort of influences on it that the run-of-the-mine physicist would have had. For that reason, I believe, there is not a single footnote in the paper that refers to anybody else's ideas. What is amazing is that the paper was accepted in that form by the Annalen der Physik, the German journal to which it was submitted. I was told that they did not have a refereeing system for papers in that journal until the 1920s. Nowadays when we submit a paper to a journal, it is sent to a referee who will want to know how your work compares to the important paper of Glich, and why you aren't citing Snerch. Pretty soon your paper becomes festooned with footnotes and you have to spend half of your life explaining why your work contradicts, or does not contradict, that of Glich and Snerch and others. In Einstein's paper there are no references to anybody, although the work bears superficial similarities to the work of other people. He felt no necessity to explain how his work was similar or different from theirs since he knew little or nothing about them.

I am nearly running out of time, so in the last couple of minutes I just want to make a few remarks about the special theory of relativity. What is most characteristic of it? Earlier work, especially that of Lorentz, was "dynamic," that is, it attempted to account for the paradoxical results of Michelson by a study of the forces involved, the dynamics. Einstein's work is what we would call "kinematic." In other words, it does not depend upon particular forces, but rather upon an analysis of the measurements of space and time. The most characteristic feature of the special theory of relativity is the analysis of time. If you think about time, you discover that when you measure the time at which an event occurs, you are really measuring the simultaneous occurrence of the event in question and that of another event, namely, the pointing of the hand of a watch, or whatever, at some particular number occurring simultaneously with the given event. Einstein recognized that the notion of time and the notion of simultaneity are intimately connected. He then understood that simultaneity is not something that is universal to all observers; what two observers at rest will call simultaneous, two observers in motion will *not* call simultaneous. Therefore, he argued by precise arguments, the concept of time for moving and resting observers should be different. In particular, a man at rest will claim that his moving counterpart has his time slowed down, which is called time dilation. This is arrived at in Einstein's special theory of relativity by general kinematic arguments involving concepts of how time is measured and by its simultaneity. Well, I don't really have time to tell you much more. Perhaps in the question period we can develop this somewhat, but Feinberg will never speak to me unless I shut up, so . . . thank you.

B. Gerald Feinberg

Dr. and Mrs. Leverton, ladies and gentlemen. It's a pleasure to be with you tonight and I'm grateful for this opportunity to be able to express in a very small way some of the homage and reverence that we physicists feel for Professor Einstein, who has certainly been a dominant figure in physics in the twentieth century. According to the division of labor that Jeremy Bernstein and I worked out, he was going to talk about relativity theory, and I would talk about the rest of Einstein's work, and so I'll begin by taking up the story in the year of 1905, when Einstein was 26, during which year, in addition to publishing his paper on the special theory of relativity, he published in the very same issue of Annalen der Physik two other papers on completely different subjects, which had perhaps equally revolutionary effects on physics. The first of the two other papers was on a subject called the Brownian Motion. I might just interpolate the remark that when Einstein died in 1955, there was a memorial meeting in New York that was addressed by a number of distinguished scientists, one of whom was Norbert Weiner, the mathematician who invented Cybernetics. During his talk Weiner made a statement to the effect that he felt that Einstein's major contribution to science was not his work on relativity or his work on the quantum theory, which is what I'm mainly going to talk about, but rather his work on Brownian Motion. I suspect he said that because Weiner's own work was, to a large extent, a follow-up on this Brownian Motion paper, but at least the comments indicate that even the things that Einstein tossed off were quite important things.

Let me say just a few words about this Brownian Motion work. What it was essentially was the first real proof of the existence of atoms. In 1905 most physicists believed that there were small things called atoms that were the ultimate constituents of matter. However, there were several quite reasonable physicists, who in fact did not believe that, who thought that there was no evidence at all for the existence of atoms, and that as a matter of fact it was impossible to find, even in principle, any existence or any evidence of existence of atoms. In this 1905 article Einstein showed that the evidence for atoms could indeed be found. He did it in a very simple way, which I might just sketch on the blackboard. His argument was the following: imagine a container with some kind of fluid in it, either a liquid or a gas. Let me imagine it's a gas, so that according to the theory of atoms there are a large number of atoms moving around inside this container. Now imagine that one suspends inside this container some kind of object. Now you can imagine that, roughly speaking, the atoms that are moving around inside the container will collide with this object. However, there are many, many atoms inside the container and they are moving in all directions. You expect that roughly the same number would hit the object from one side as from the other, so that there would be no particular tendency for the object to move in any direction, that for every atom that hits it from one side, another atom would hit it from the other side, and the object would more or less remain at rest. Einstein noticed, apparently for the first time, in 1905, that whereas it is true on the average that equal numbers of atoms hit the object in all directions, it is not true at any instant. At any instant, say, one atom will hit the object and will make the object move a little bit in one direction and then at the next instant another atom will hit it from a different side and the object will move a little bit in another direction, and so on. What Einstein then did was to show, on the basis of this very simple argument, that a small object suspended in fluid, such as a liquid, would be expected to have a kind of jittery motion. In this motion it would not move straight in some direction; instead it would jiggle back and forth. By looking at such an object under the microscope, you should be able to see this motion. What he was able to do was to figure out how much the motion should be, based on how big the atoms were, and so on. Now, interestingly enough, the fact that small objects suspended in a liquid undergo a motion of that kind was discovered one hundred years or so before Einstein wrote this article, and indeed was called Brownian Motion, because the man who discovered it was named Brown. In the intervening one hundred years, apparently nobody thought that there might be a relationship between this phenomenon and the existence of atoms. While Einstein did realize it, he apparently didn't know, at least when he started to work, that the Brownian Motion had been observed. In other words, he was making a prediction. At the end of the article of 1905, he says something like somebody told me that this has actually already been observed, as indeed it had been. So that was Einstein's contribution to proving that atoms exist, and once he published this, almost all the people who had been skeptical about atoms were convinced.

The other thing that Einstein did in 1905 was to make a decisive contribution to what is known as "quantum theory." Quantum theory is seventy-five years old this year. The first article on it was written by a man named Planck in December of 1900, so next month it will be seventy-five years old; and the complete form of the quantum theory, which sometimes goes under the name of quantum mechanics, was invented fifty years ago, in August of 1925, by a then young man by the name of Werner Heissenberg, who is still alive. [Heissenberg died in 1976.]

Einstein's contributions to the quantum theory came in three stages, which I might list formally, because I think it's interesting to keep them in mind. Stage A lasted roughly between the years 1905 and 1920. The years 1905 to 1920 might be called Einstein's creative period, in that he made several original discoveries about the quantum theory, some of which I will describe in a bit more detail. The second period, from roughly 1920 to 1930, might be referred to as his advisory period. During those years Einstein himself did not make any very original discoveries in quantum theory. However, he did in this period recognize the importance of several discoveries made by other scientists, and he helped to bring them to the attention of the rest of the scientific community, and in addition, as I'll mention later on, he apparently played an important role in stimulating a major advance in quantum theory made in this period by Heissenberg. Finally, between the period of 1930 and his death in 1955, there was what I call Einstein's critical period in regard to quantum theory. In that period, although almost all physicists were happy with the version of quantum theory that had been developed, Einstein himself was not at all satisfied with it, and instead of using it in his work, he tried to show that it was actually not a satisfactory theory at all, which is why I refer to this as his critical period.

In spite of the fact that Einstein had a great deal to do with the quantum theory, I think it is fair to say that in none of these periods was the quantum theory Einstein's main interest. I think that his main interest in physics was the theory of relativity, first in the form that Professor Bernstein has described, the special theory of relativity, and later on, in the years between 1915 and 1920, what is called the general theory of relativity or the theory of gravitation. I think that is what Einstein regarded as the center of his scientific work. As for quantum theory, although it was tremendously important, I think it was probably not what he was mainly interested in. On the other hand, from the point of view of myself and, I think, most other physicists, the quantum theory does represent the major intellectual accomplishment of the human race in the twentieth century. So we are quite happy that Einstein did what he did for the development of the quantum theory.

Let me then begin by describing very briefly the 1905 work of Einstein on the quantum theory. Before this work there was really only one article written on the quantum theory, the one that I mentioned by Planck in 1900, and it is interesting that whereas in Einstein's relativity papers in 1905 he had no references at all to other people's work, in the quantum theory paper he did refer the work of Planck. Now that is interesting, because nobody else referred to the

work of Planck in those years, so that Einstein's knowledge
of other people's work, at least the extent to which he was
willing to refer to it, was somewhat erratic. In some cases
he gave credit to people whom nobody else did, and in other
cases he didn't give people credit, because he didn't know
about them. The thing that Planck had done in 1900 was
to show that the emission and absorption of light by matter
took place not in a continuous way, but rather in what we
now think of as a discrete way. That is to say, when light is
emitted or absorbed by objects, the amount of energy carried
off by the light comes in little bits, which Planck called
"quanta," in such a way that light of any particular color—
red light, blue light, and so on—comes in these little bits
of energy, which one might think of as little particles.
Furthermore, for light of any color, the particles each have
a definite amount of energy; particles of red light have one
amount of energy, particles of blue light have a different
amount of energy, etcetera. Planck showed that, based on
this idea, it was possible to understand the way that bodies
emitted light when they were heated up to various temperatures. There had been careful measurements of how bodies
of different temperatures emitted light and Planck showed
that, based on this idea, light came in little bundles of energy.
You can understand how that worked. In Einstein's work in
1905, he followed up on this idea, using a branch of physics
that goes under the name of statistical thermodynamics.
Now, the fact that he used statistical thermodynamics is
itself interesting for the following reason: before Einstein's
papers in 1905, he had written several others on physics in
1902 and 1903, and in some of those papers he invented this
subject that I refer to: statistical thermodynamics. That is,
he wrote several papers in which he worked out the theory
that we now call statistical thermodynamics. Now, ordi-
narily, one would have thought that this by itself would have

made him a great reputation as a physicist. The only trouble was that statistical thermodynamics had been invented by two other people some years earlier. It was invented by a European physicist named Boltzmann and an American physicist named Gibbs. Einstein's work on statistical thermodynamics was almost identical to the work of Gibbs. The only trouble is that he did it two or three years later, without knowing that Gibbs had done it beforehand. Actually, the way Enstein did it was in some ways better than the way Gibbs did it, but given the way scientists assign credit for things, the person who does it first usually gets the credit for it, and so Einstein's reputation was not made by his work on statistical thermodynamics, even though it was a major accomplishment to do it without knowing that other people had done it independently. In any case, Einstein did use these inventions of statistical thermodynamics to analyze further the ideas that Planck had introduced, and he showed first of all that, according to these notions, light was not only emitted and absorbed in these discrete bundles of energy called quanta, but actually, under all circumstances, even when the light was simply moving through space, it would again have to be in the form of these discrete quanta, which later came to be known as photons. Einstein went on in this very same article to do something that had not been done before, which was to use this idea that light comes in discrete quanta to explain a new physical phenomenon that had been known for a while before but had not been explained. That phenomenon goes under the name of photoemission, and it means roughly the following: if you have a clean metal surface and you shine light on it, you find that under certain circumstances the metal surface will begin to emit electrical particles called electrons, so that if you attached a wire to the surface, you could actually get a flow of electricity out of it. Now, it was known for about twenty years before

Einstein did his work that for some specific metal surface this would happen for only certain kinds of light. It might happen for, say, blue light, but not for red light. Furthermore, it would still happen even if the light that you shone on it was very, very feeble; in other words, there didn't have to be very much light to do this. Those two facts, that this photoemission could happen with very feeble light sources, and that it depended on the color of the light, were known before Einstein, but they were not understood, and Einstein was able to show, using this idea of Planck, that one can understand this kind of photoemission directly on the basis of the idea that light comes in those little bundles of energy called quanta.

I am not going to explain to you the reasoning that he went through to prove this. Not the least of the reasons for my not doing it is that it's very difficult for even a modern physicist to understand the reasoning he performed. In fact, when I read his article for the first time, I was reminded very much of a passage in Homer's *Iliad*, which I copied out to read to you in rough English translation. This is in book five of the *Iliad*, and the passage goes: "But the son of Tydeus caught up a mighty stone, so huge and great, that as men now are, it would take two to lift it. Nevertheless, he bore it aloft with ease unaided." This indicates that the methods that Einstein used in his 1905 article on the photo-effect are things that nowadays physicists are simply not able to do. The kind of training we receive now is not at all the kind of training that some of the people like Planck and Einstein received then, and not only are we not easily able to reproduce their arguments, but it is even hard for us to understand them. This doesn't mean that we don't have our own ways of understanding these things, it just means that we have a different approach to them. However, whatever method he used, Einstein was able to come to the right conclusion that the photoeffect was connected with the existence of light quanta. This was Einstein's first important contribution to quantum theory in 1905. In the ten years that followed he made a few minor contributions to quantum theory—that is, minor for him; for anybody else they would have made his reputation, but for Einstein they were minor contributions. He showed that this idea that energy came in discrete bundles rather than in a continuous distribution could be applied not only to light, but also to certain other phenomena, and he used it to explain some properties of matter, such as how much the temperature of a piece of matter increases when you add a certain amount of heat to it.

But in this period, as I mentioned earlier, Einstein's major interest was in the general theory of relativity, which he completed in 1916. Now, perhaps as a result of having completed the general theory of relativity, Einstein in 1917 again focused his attention for a while on the quantum theory, and he made another major contribution to it, this time having to do with the interaction of light and other kinds of radiation with matter. I will again summarize what he did very briefly. Let's again imagine a closed container with atoms in it, but now let's imagine that these atoms are all emitting and absorbing light. That atoms emit and absorb light was known for a long time, and several years before 1917, in the work of the physicist Neils Bohr, a certain understanding of how individual atoms emit and absorb light was reached. Now, what Einstein did in 1917 was the following: if we have a closed container with atoms in it that are emitting light and absorbing light, one can show that after a while, in addition to the atoms that are in the container, there is a certain amount of light in the container that is in equilibrium with the atoms. By that I just mean that the amount of light does not change after a while, and the distribution of atoms among their states does not change after a while either. Einstein was able to show that this conclusion, that an equilibrium would be reached between the light and the matter, with a particular kind of distribution of the light, followed from some very simple ideas—the ideas that the individual emission and absorption of light by the atoms happened at random, that is to say, the time or place at which any given atom would emit the light or absorb the light was not determined by anything, but happened randomly. The only thing that was not random was this: since any particular atom could either emit light or absorb light, there had to be a certain relationship between the probability of the atom's emitting light and the probability of its absorbing light, which relationship he wrote down. Furthermore, he had to make an additional assumption, which is that if an atom is hit by one of these light quanta that I mentioned earlier, it might not only absorb the light quantum, but it was possible for the atom also to do something that Einstein called "stimulated emission," which means that instead of having one quantum come in and none go out, one quantum comes in and two go out. In other words, having one light quantum hit the atom might make the atom emit a second light quantum rather than absorb the first one. This is his "stimulated emission."

Fifty years later, in the 1960s, this notion of stimulated emission came to play a very important role in technology through the invention of what we now call the laser. The word *laser* is an acronym that stands for *light amplification* by *stimulated emission* of *radiation*. So this original idea of Einstein of stimulated emission, after fifty years, became a technological miracle, so to speak, and was directly involved in the invention of the laser.

People sometimes give Einstein credit for the atomic bomb by saying that his equation E equals MC squared is what was used in building the atomic bomb. That is a somewhat exaggerated statement. There is really very little relation between the two. On the other hand, there is a very close relation between the invention of stimulated emission and the work in the laser, so really it would be better to give Einstein credit for the laser than to give him credit for the atomic bomb.

With that 1917 paper, Einstein's creative period in quantum theory more or less came to an end. He did some other work in it, but nothing quite so important as what he had done before.

Let me now turn to the second period, during which quantum theory was undergoing very important changes and becoming a complete physical theory. In that period, as I said, Einstein was the first to recognize the importance of certain ideas that had been proposed by other physicists, including the French scientist Louis Debroglie, and the Indian scientist Bose. But because he was Einstein, just having him say that this was an important idea automatically got other people to pay attention to it and got these ideas into the mainstream of physics much more quickly than would have happened otherwise. In recent years there has come to light in an autobiographical statement by Heissenberg an indication that Einstein also played an advisory role in Heissenberg's work, in particular the formulation of what has come to be known as Heissenberg's uncertainty principle. This principle is a relation in quantum mechanics governing the amount of information that can be obtained about two different quantities at the same time in its most direct form. It says, for instance, that while you can measure the position of an atom or the speed of an atom at any given time, you cannot measure both the position and the speed of the atom at the same time, at least not accurately. In the autobiographical statement I mentioned, Heissenberg said that in a conversation he had had with Einstein a year or so before he came out with the uncertainty relation, Einstein suggested to him that what can be observed in science is decided by each physical theory; in other words, what can be observed is not something you can decide independently of physical theory, but you have to know what the physical theory you are talking about *is* before you know what can be observed. Heissenberg says that this conversation gave him the clue to the correct way to formulate the uncertainty principle. Interestingly enough, the uncertainty principle was done in 1927. Approximately three years later, in 1930, there was a conference, one of a series called the Solvay Conferences, in Belgium, I think, at which Einstein and Heissenberg and other scientists were present, and in the course of this conference there were several interesting discussions between Einstein and another eminent scientist of the period, Niels Bohr, on this uncertainty principle. These conversations are recorded, for those who might be interested in them, in an article by Bohr in a book called *Albert Einstein: Philosopher-Scientist*, edited by P. Schilpp and published in 1949. This book also has a series of articles on Einstein's life and work by various physicists, as well as an autobiographical statement by Einstein about his own life and work. Bohr indicates in his article that in these conversations between him and Einstein, Einstein was extremely critical of the uncertainty principle, although according to Heissenberg, he stimulated it, and that Einstein tried very hard to show that there was something wrong with the principle, that there was a way of getting around it. Bohr had to work very hard, each time Einstein suggested another possible flaw in it, to try to figure why the criticism was invalid. He gives several examples of how that procedure went. This was perhaps one of the earliest indications of how critical Einstein was going to be of this final version of quantum mechanics, and he then went on to continue this criticism. The thing that seemed to bother Einstein most about quantum mechanics was the fact that the theory of quantum mechanics, unlike all previous theories in physics, is not a deterministic one. That is to say, quantum mechanics doesn't enable you to make exact predictions of *when* things are going to happen. What it does enable you to do is to make predictions of the relative probability of things happening, but not to make exact predictions. For example, according to quantum mechanics an individual atom may emit radiation at any time in any place, but the theory doesn't enable you to predict when a particular atom will do that. But it does enable you to say that, if you have a large number of atoms in a big sample of matter, these will emit radiation statistically in a certain regular way. For example, if you have 10^{23} atoms, then half of them will emit radiation in some period of time, and then half the remaining ones will emit radiation in another period of time, and so on. But it cannot determine when any individual atom will do it. It's a little bit like being able to say that if you flip a coin a million times, it will almost certainly come down approximately five hundred thousand times heads and five hundred thousand tails. But if you flip it one time, you cannot say whether it will come down heads or tails. Einstein believed that the time at which any individual atom emits radiation is really determined in advance and that there would be some future theory, which he didn't specify, that would allow us to predict when this would happen, even though the quantum theory did not. Einstein believed this until he died in 1955. The developments in the twenty years since his death have not given any indication that he was correct in this, that is, we have not found any theory that would enable us to make these predictions about what individual atoms do, and furthermore, there have been advances in our experimental techniques over that period that enable us to really study what individual atoms or individual subatomic particles do. In making those studies, we found that even for certain subatomic particles that do not seem to have any kind of complicated structure such as atoms are now known to have, the individual subatomic particles still do decay at random as far as we can tell, in just the way the quantum mechanics suggests they do. So if Einstein is correct in his belief that quantum mechanics will eventually be replaced by something else, we have not been able to find the replacement yet. I think it's fair to say that most physicists believe that we never will find that kind of replacement.

I thought I might conclude by making a remark about what one does in the face of disagreements between physicists such as that between Einstein on the one hand, and most of the other physicists on the other hand, about the quantum theory. There are several possible attitudes one can take. One attitude is to believe that Einstein was correct, and that the rest of us have just been misled by the successes of quantum theory to think that it is the right theory, but that in reality it is not the right theory. As I said, very few physicists take that view; a few do, but it's not at all a common one. Another point of view one can take is that Einstein was simply wrong, that although he was instrumental in the early days of quantum theory, he eventually went off on the wrong track. The fact that he didn't believe in quantum theory is hard luck. I think that perhaps the best alternative, however, was expressed in an article by physicist Max Born that also appeared in *Albert Einstein: Philosopher-Scientist*. I might read just a couple of lines from that article. Born says about Einstein:

He has seen more clearly than anyone before him the statistical background of the laws of physics, and he was a pioneer in the struggle for conquering the wilderness of the quantum phenomena. Yet later, when out of his own work, a synthesis of statistical and quantum principle emerged, which seemed to be acceptable to all physicists, he kept himself aloof and skeptical. Many of us regard this as a tragedy; for him as he groped his way in loneliness, and for us who miss our leader and standard bearer. But in spite of this, he remains our beloved master.

Thank you.

DR. ANGOFF: Thank you very much, Dr. Feinberg and Dr. Bernstein. You have made life enormously more fascinating tonight than it has been before. I'm bewildered, but I'm also fascinated. I also would like to say before you people decide on what questions to ask, how much encouragement they have given some of us. Einstein never would have made the Dean's List at Fairleigh Dickinson. I also doubt very much if he could have passed the college entrance examinations, and he would probably have been put on probation. So the lesson is: Never sneer at people who look like schnooks or "schnookesses," because there may be an Einstein hidden beneath. Okay. And now for some questions:

Q.: Is there anyone who is actively pursuing the deterministic point of view? It seems like an example of the fractions of the times to accept the premise that matter behaves in a random way. Couldn't it be as valid an approach to assume the opposite and investigate along those lines?

Did you all hear the question? The question is, Does matter behave in a helter-skelter manner, or does it behave in a deterministic manner? Is that right? "Not quite, I was just wondering if anyone is actively pursuing this?"

A.: Yes. There are a few people who are trying to make deterministic theory of subatomic phenomena. They're not getting anywhere, in my opinion, but they are trying to do it.

My own point of view, for what it's worth, is that it is remarkable we can learn anything at all about subatomic phenomena, and we shouldn't be surprised that we can't learn as much about them as we can about everyday phenomena, so that I, at least, feel comfortable with the fact that they seem to behave at random. There are people who follow Einstein who are not happy with that and who try to modify the quantum theory in various ways to make it deterministic. As far as I know, none of these approaches has led to any new ideas or predictions that seem to work out. People will probably continue to try it.

Q.:   It seems there is a new subatomic particle discovered every time I read your magazine. In your opinion, is there any limit to the smallness with which matter can exist? Are there an infinite number of onionskins here?

A.:   My opinion is that there are not, but I think it's not worth very much as an opinion.

Q.:   There are not an infinite number?

A.:   No, there are *not* an infinite number.

Q.:   This question is for Dr. Bernstein. Do you see any similarity between Einstein's way of looking at the universe, and the way the Eastern mind looks at the universe?

A.:   When one speaks of Einstein's way of looking at the universe, I think one has to separate two things. On the one hand, he was a deeply religious, almost mystically religious, human being; and on the other hand, he was a scientist. In his view of the universe as a scientist, his concern was ultimately to make predictions that had precise numerical consequences that could be verified experimentally. In this sense he was, I think, in no way like an Eastern mystic. This kind of prediction is not their concern. On the other hand, in his belief in the unity and simplicity of nature and in his deep religious sense, maybe he did have some resemblance. I know he had a great sympathy toward and an appreciation of some Indian religious mystics. He was an admirer of Gandhi and an admirer of Tagore, and I think he appreciated their way of looking at things, but I think you have to separate this from his working method as a physicist.

Q.: This is for Dr. Bernstein. I don't know if you used the word *contempt* in the very beginning to describe his reaction to having a stomach and toward revealing personal things . . .

A.: Well, *contempt*, I think, was the wrong word. I think that he would have preferred not to have a stomach. *Contempt* was the wrong word, I should have used *disdain*. In that sense, I think he is different from most people, because I think most people are not unhappy about having stomachs. We enjoy food and eating and so on, and for many people it is an important part of life. I think that for him there was a disdain for that kind of human thing.

Q.: You said in his autobiography what his stomach forces him to do—to earn a living—and that that's what his disdain was for.

A.: I am at a great disadvantage for not having known the man, but I did have a chance to visit his house in Princeton at 112 Mercer Street, and I did see the apartment he had earlier lived in in the latter part of his life. It was very austere. It had not been much changed from what it was during his lifetime. I do not think that it is the kind of place that most people would have chosen to live and work in. It was serene, but very austere, rather plain. I wouldn't go so far as to say it was a dormitory room, but it had a little bit of that effect on me.

DR. ANGOFF: I can add something to that. I knew a woman, Ruth Norden, who used to translate his German articles into English. Did you ever come across her? She told me something I've always remembered, I don't know why. He loved bananas and apricots. I don't know, maybe that's a contribution.

Q.: Could a stimulated emission add energy to the world?

A.:   In the form that it is in the laser, what it does is not add energy to the world, but transform energy from one form into another. What the laser does, more or less, is to take the unorganized form of energy, in which there are a lot of different colors, each of which has a certain amount of energy, and by using this stimulated emission process, it transforms it all into energy of one kind. I don't see how you could get new energy by using stimulated emission, because energy is conserved in the process. What happens when an atom is hit by a photon, is that in order for it to undergo stimulated emission, the atom must already be in a higher energy state than it is normally in, and then that higher energy of the atom is converted into the energy of the photon it emits. So you are just getting the energy from the atom into the energy of the photon. In order for that to work, though, you have to, at the outset, give the atom enough energy to bring it into that higher energy state. So I don't see that you gain anything by it. You might be able to use the energy in a better form that way, as the laser does.

Q.:   Why did Einstein use the name *relativity* to describe his theory?

A.:   From what I can gather, this was not Einstein's first choice. From what I understand from Professor Holton of Harvard, who is an expert on the history of the relativity theory, Einstein wanted to call it the theory of invariants. In fact, the relativity theory paper is not callel the relativity theory paper, it is called "On the Elective Dynamics of Moving Bodies." So it is something of an accident that the word *relativity* got into it at all. In some ways it is rather a pity that it did, because *relativity* has been taken to mean all sorts and kinds of things that were not intended. It is a word that has got into the literature, and I think one should not allow oneself to be trapped by the word. It just means that certain concepts such as length and time, electric field, and so on must be specified relative to a coordinate system in order for them to have a meaning.

Q.:   Can you say something about the "Twin Paradox"?

A.:   I'll just say a word or two about the twins, first of all, for those of you who don't know what the so-called twin paradox is. Let me explain what it is because it is very, very interesting. First, let us forget about human twins. Let's rather talk about two identical clocks or oscillators. Now, the statement is the following: imagine one of these clocks or oscillators sitting at rest here, and send the other oscillator on a round trip, then the oscillator that takes the trip will emit *fewer* beats, according to the observers that stay home, than the resting oscillator. Sometimes this is put in a very dramatic way by saying that a traveling twin remains younger, that the heart has emitted fewer beats. Now, this part of the thing nobody who has understood the relativity theory has any trouble with. It follows from a straightforward calculation. Trouble comes when someone asks, What if one describes this from the point of view of the traveling twin? Now, naively one might say that the two situations should be equivalent. Therefore the moving twin would claim that the resting twin is also younger, and therefore, one would have a paradox. The true situation is not equivalent because the resting twin has rested, and the moving twin has been acted on by forces. The two situations are simply not equivalent. Therefore, in fact, if one does the calculation correctly and carefully, one finds that *both* men will agree that the *moving* twin, the twin that has been accelerated, will be younger. There is no contradiction.

DR. ANGOFF: I'd like to ask a question. I've always been puzzled by a seeming contradiction in Einstein. Time and again he said, "I have no religion," but he also said, I believe,

"I do not believe this world is the result of a throw of dice."
Now once you say that, you subsume a plan, isn't that right?
Can you enlighten me?

DR. BERNSTEIN: I give that to Feinberg!

DR. FEINBERG: Well, I think his remark about not believing
that God throws dice was specifically a reference to this
thing that I mentioned, not believing that things were in-
determinate. That is, he believed that eventually we would
know exactly how everything happened. The aphorism is
a sort of a graphic way of saying that. As for Einstein's religious belief as such, I recall in one of his autobiographical
statements that he said something about believing in Spinoza's God, rather than in a personal one. I'm not expert
enough on Spinoza to be able to tell what exactly he had in
mind, but he did seem to have some views along those lines.

DR. ANGOFF: Thank you very much, Dr. Bernstein and
Dr. Feinberg, for adding to our delight in being alive. We
have learned a great deal. We shall always remember it and
thank you for coming.

New Jersey's Contributions to the Chemical Industry and Chemical Education

The Program

Introductory Speakers

Dr. Saul K. Fenster

Dr. Charles Angoff

Dr. Irvin M. Citron

Main Speakers

Dr. Henry B. Hass

Dr. A. K. Bose

Topic   New Jersey's Contributions to the Chemical Industry and Chemical Education

The Participants

Dr. Henry B. Hass has had more than half a century of experience in chemistry. He is a past Chairperson of the Chemistry Department at Purdue University. Dr. Hass has served as Research and Development Director of GAF and M. W. Kellogg Companies. He is past President of the Sugar Research Foundation. A Ph.D. graduate of Ohio State University, he was awarded the coveted Perkin Medal. His research into nitro-alkanes resulted in the development of propellants for the Polaris missiles.

Dr. A. K. Bose earned his Sc.D. at the Massachusetts Institute of Technology, and also did post-doctoral work at Harvard University with Dr. Woodward, a Nobel Prize winner. He has been Professor of Chemistry at Stevens Institute since 1959. He is a recipient of the Otten Award for excellence in research at Stevens Institute, and he is a fellow of the New York Academy of Sciences.

Dr. Saul K. Fenster is Professor of Mechanical Engineering and Provost of the Rutherford Campus of Fairleigh Dickinson University.

DR. CHARLES ANGOFF is Professor Emeritus of English at the Rutherford Campus of Fairleigh Dickinson University and is the Leverton Lecture Series Chairperson in Rutherford.

DR. IRVIN M. CITRON is Professor of Chemistry at the Rutherford Campus of Fairleigh Dickinson University and currently Chemistry Department Chairperson there. He is the coordinator of this evening's program.

New Jersey's Contributions to the Chemical Industry and Chemical Education

A. Henry B. Hass

DR. FENSTER: Welcome to the Rutherford Campus and to tonight's episode in the Leverton Lecture Series, a very significant contribution to the cultural and educational life of the University. I would like to introduce to you Mr. and Mrs. Morris Leverton, our benefactors. There is a very brief biographical sketch of the Levertons at the beginning of the book. I just want to say that to know the Levertons is to know that we have here people who are extremely gentle people, kind and generous, and who love both the students and the University, which of course are part and parcel of the same thing. Mr. and Mrs. Leverton. We thank you very much.

Now I would like to introduce you to Dr. Charles Angoff, professor emeritus of English Literature. Dr. Angoff, distinguished scholar, writer, poet, novelist, author of forty books, editor of the FDU Press and *The Literary Review*.

Charles, who is the Chairman of the Leverton Lecture Series for the Rutherford Campus, had much to do with the arranging of these lectures. Charles entertains me occasionally over the radio waves as I drive between Rutherford and Teaneck. One of the fringe benefits of being part of a tri-campus university is to be in a vehicle for at least part of your life, one-third, one-quarter, one-eighth, depending on the week, and every so often around the noon hour or one o'clock I hear Charlie reading poetry over WNYC, and it makes that trip between Rutherford and Route 17 to Teaneck—which as you know is not really the most aesthetically pleasant trip in the world—it makes that trip a pleasure and a joy. I've heard him reading his poetry many times and it has inspired me to read his poetry, and it gives me a great pleasure to introduce Dr. Charles Angoff.

DR. ANGOFF: Thank you very much, Dr. Fenster. I am the Chairman of the Leverton Lecture Series in Rutherford; the other three people on the Committee are Dr. Harvey Bird, Professor of Physics, Dr. Richard Klosek, Professor of Biological Sciences, and Dr. Jean Willis, Professor of History. The Leverton Lectures in Rutherford for the past four years have been devoted entirely to a consideration of the contributions of New Jersey to the national culture on all major levels—in literature, in music, in painting, in ecology, in statesmanship, in physics. I say New Jersey. New Jersey is a small state; it is hedged in between two giants, Pennsylvania and New York. Winston Churchill spoke of that tight little island England. He could also have spoken of that tight little state New Jersey. It's a little state, but it's been very great in its contributions to culture. Apparently the good Lord is partial to little things. Remember that Palestine, now Israel, was very small when it produced its three major religions. Greece was very small; Athens in its heyday probably had no more than twenty-five thousand people. Consider now Denmark, Holland, Norway, Sweden, Venice, Bavaria. I mention Venice and Bavaria for a special reason. When they were independent states, they were very great contributors of culture, but then when they were swallowed up—by Italy in the case of Venice, and by Germany in the case of Bavaria—they became, intellectually speaking, largely deserts. Some people have said that perhaps the good Lord also likes small women. I don't know; I am ecumenical when it comes to that matter.

Today we are going to consider New Jersey's contribution in the realm of chemistry, both as philosophy and as applied science. I'm a little bit embarrassed to talk to you now about chemistry, because I know nothing about it. When I went to Harvard, I studied chemistry with Professor Theodore W. Richards, a Nobel Prize winner. I got an A, but I didn't know a thing. I also studied with Professor Bridgeman, who got a Nobel Prize in Physics, and I didn't know a thing. There's a trick to getting an A in a subject that you don't understand. I can get an A in Egyptian Hieroglyphics if called upon to do so. So I'm going to listen extra carefully tonight; maybe I will learn something. Fortunately, we have two speakers who really know the subject, and they will be introduced by the Chairman of the Chemistry Department at Rutherford, who also knows the subject extremely well, Dr. Irvin Citron. Dr. Citron.

DR. CITRON: I thank you. I'm flattered that Dr. Angoff thinks I know a little bit about chemistry. We are indeed fortunate to have two prominent speakers here who have participated greatly in the advancement of chemistry, chemical industry, and chemical education in the state of New Jersey. Unfortunately, one of the original speakers that we had intended to have here this evening has been unable to attend because of a personal problem in his family, and he graciously got one of his colleagues to come here in his place. Dr. Pollara, who could not attend, got Dr. Bose, who is a very well-known organic chemist in Stevens Institute of Technology, the same University that Dr. Pollara teaches at, and he has graciously consented to come here and fill in for Dr. Pollara. I am sure you will get the same benefit out of Dr. Bose's talk, and you will be none the worse for wear. As Dr. Angoff mentioned, as a state New Jersey has often been sort of lost between New York and Pennsylvania. We sometimes do not get credit for the things that happen in this state, and I think that this has lately been brought to the fore very succinctly. For example, the other day when I was riding home in the car, I found out that New Jersey is going to get credit for something, and guess what it is? I heard the announcer say it has been suggested that the Swine Flu, since it originated at Fort Dix, New Jersey, should be renamed "New Jersey Flu." So maybe we'll make the map after all, but after all, there have been a number of incidents, a number of events in New Jersey, in chemistry, in chemical education, and in the cultural arts—and in many other aspects of human endeavor that have been very notable, and some people overlook this. Some other people have been given credit for things that have been done in this vicinity. The speakers tonight, I am sure, will help clear this up. Our first speaker, Dr. Henry Hass, is the former chairman of the Chemistry Department at Purdue University; he has been a research and development director at GAF and the M. W. Kellogg Companies; he is past president of the Sugar Research Foundation; he has done much research into nitroalkanes and helped develop the propellants for the Polaris missile. His Ph.D. was acquired at Ohio State University; he has been associated in his work in New Jersey with numerous educational institutions, and he is active in the American

Chemical Society and also in the American Institute of Chemists. He has also been the recipient of one of the most coveted medals in chemistry, the Perkin medal for outstanding achievement in chemistry. I have the great honor to introduce to you Dr. Hass.

DR. HASS: Ladies and gentlemen, it was with great pleasure that I learned that there is another poet here. Writing light verse is one of my hobbies, and this evening I would like to tell you about my old friend Earl Butz:

At old Purdue, I knew Earl Butz, a man we all applaud.
His friends are happy his parents didn't call him Claude.
And Harry is another name his parents never used,
Which shows that they were on the ball, and not at all
    confused.
When Butz had been professor there, for twenty-five long
    years,
His friends assembled in a group and raised some happy
    cheers.
They gave him then an ashtray like a tiny toilet seat;
The words "For Butz" were printed there in letters small
    and neat.

Before I allowed that poem to reach the light of day, I wrote to my old friend Earl, to whom I taught freshman Chemistry, and said, if you find this offensive, I will throw it in the wastepaper basket. He wrote back no, that people with names like mine should expect such things, and it reminded me of my imaginary brother Seymour, who is a dress designer in Paris, where the letter H is not pronounced. As you have already guessed, he made his reputation on miniskirts and hot pants. That's the end of the poetry, as far as I'm concerned this evening.

I would now like to tell you about some chemical achievements that occurred in the state of New Jersey. First, I should point out that the greatest concentration of chemists that exists anywhere in the world is right here in northern New Jersey. The North Jersey section of the American Chemical Society has seven thousand members, which is larger even than the New York section; and there are probably about an equal number of chemists who don't belong to the American Chemical Society in this vicinity. Obviously, nobody can speak of all of the achievements of chemistry in New Jersey. I had to use some criterion for the eight true stories that I am going to tell. The criterion that I used was that only things having a multibillion-dollar impact are the things I'm going to talk about this evening.

I want to begin with the story of a man who got the idea that there ought to be some way of making celluloid—which he named—without using solvents. Now, celluloid was not new to him as a product, but solvents had always been used to combine the cellulose nitrate and the camphor; what happened then was that as the solvents evaporated, the volume of it decreased, and all was irregular because the volume decreased more on the outside than on the inside, because the outside was where the solvent evaporated first. And so the things made out of celluloid before Mr. Hyatt's time were apt to come out of the factory all bent, and not the shape they were supposed to be. Then he got a very courageous idea. Cellulose nitrate, you understand, is what they put in cartridges to make the bullets come out of the gun. It's a propellant explosive. And it's not very stable chemically, really. He got the idea of taking cellulose nitrate, grinding it to a fine powder—that took some courage right there—then mixing it with the camphor, also ground into a fine powder, and after mixing them, putting the heat and pressure on, enough to melt the camphor. Maybe then he wouldn't have to use another solvent at all. Well, he knew this was dangerous, as I read recently in the description of how he did the experiment. He took a two-inch plank and put it between him and the potential erplosive when he turned on the heat and pressure. Now, if he'd been unlucky he would have ended up with splinters all through his body, but fortunately it didn't explode. And that was the beginning of the great industrial development of celluloid, which was the first commercially successful plastic. And that happened right here in New Jersey, and the first plant was built in New Jersey. After a while, it burned down, because they were dealing with a dangerous material. But they built another, larger one, they made a lot of money from it, and it was important in its own right. I remember, when we were young boys, that the poor people who couldn't afford to send their collars to the laundry would wear celluloid collars, because they could take soap and water and scrub them off and they were as good as new. Well, that started the whole plastics industry, and I don't have to explain, even to a nontechnical audience, about the importance of plastics. And that began right here in the state of New Jersey.

My second story is located in Summit, New Jersey, where I happen to live. Around the corner from me when I moved to Summit was a man by the name of Williams, Robert Williams. He was a very interesting chap to know. His parents had been missionaries in the Orient, and he had learned there that people who ate polished rice often got beriberi; people who ate unpolished rice just never got beriberi. You might wonder why people might be so stupid as to eat polished rice. Well, it was a mark of social distinction to eat polished rice because it was more expensive than unpolished rice. When I was in the Philippines, they told me about a sugar central there where they didn't want their employees to get beriberi, so they wouldn't keep polished rice in the company store. Most of the workmen were so poor, always buying more than they should, that they were always behind in their payments and the only place they could get credit was the company store. But they never got beriberi because they weren't able to buy polished rice there—with one exception. There was a Chinese accountant there, and he was making more money than the rest of them, and he could afford to go outside the company store and buy polished rice. He came down with beriberi. My friend Robert Williams decided that there was something lost in the rice polishings that was a nutritional factor that prevented beriberi. Now it seems sort of obvious, doesn't it, but for a while people didn't even believe there were nutritional deficiency diseases. He got some rice polishings—which they were always feeding to the chickens—and the chickens just grew fine—and extracted them and got a crystalline material that he tried on experimental animals. That was what he called the "beriberi vitamin." Well, that would have been a great achievement if he had stopped right there; but he didn't. He went ahead and determined the structure of this material, which at that time was a difficult thing to do—which atoms are there, which atoms are combined with which other atoms, in which arrangement in space? That all had to be determined, and he did it. And then he synthesized the stuff, and that's why he got a Perkin medal. That was put into commercial operation by Merck, another New Jersey outfit, and then someone down at Merck got a bright idea: if you can make vitamin B_1, as we call it now, why couldn't you make the other vitamins synthetically too? They got a lot of very bright chemists, worked very hard, and now all the important vitamins can be made synthetically—not some cheap imitation of the natural product but identical with the natural product, and that is why vitamins have become readily available and cheap, and everybody who has any kind of a steady job at all or any source of income at all can have all the vitamins he wants. So what is the impact of that? Why do

I put that in the multibillion-dollar-impact category? Well, Sherman, up at Columbia, had shown with rats that, if you take litter mates and divide them into two equal groups, and do that with a great many litter mates, then you have rats that are strictly comparable in the two groups. You raise one group on a diet that for many generations has been proved to be perfectly adequate nutritionally. To the other rats you give the same diet, except that you give them extra vitamins. And what happens? Four things: first, the rats in the second group mature more rapidly; second, they get larger; third, they have less disease; and fourth, they live longer. And Sherman said that people are enough like rats so that we can believe that this is what is going to happen to people if they eat extra vitamins. The medical profession —which I don't want to criticize, for I have a son and a daughter-in-law who are both MD's, and they are wonderful people—the medical profession in this country is more lined up to cure disease than to prevent it. There are still people who don't believe in extra vitamins, but fortunately or unfortunately, the average housewife is not among these people. And so the kids of this country have been getting extra vitamins for about thirty or forty years now, thanks primarily to this development, first with Robert Williams, then at Merck. So what has happened? Well, as you know, we lowered the voting age from twenty-one to eighteen recently. Why? That's what Sherman found, wasn't it, with rats? Quicker maturity. The kids are bigger. I had an uncle who was captain of his football team and weighed one hundred eighty pounds and played tackle. Nowadays, one hundred eighty pounds is hardly big enough to play quarterback. We are bigger than we used to be. We are living longer; that has caught up already on the vital statistics. And we have less disease, just the way Sherman said it would be. And this all happened in the wonderful state of New Jersey.

My next story has to do with the first truly synthetic fiber. That is the first synthetic fiber to be built up from small molecules by fastening them together end to end into a long, string-shaped molecule. Prior to the work on nylon, which I am going to talk about, there had been synthetic fibers made by taking natural fibers and modifying them along the line of the string-shaped molecule. I'm not talking about that; I'm talking about building them up from scratch from small molecules. The first one was nylon, and this resulted from the genius of a fellow by the name of Carothers, a laboratory man, followed by work by E. K. Bolton and his group, who drove the process through pilot plant and into commercial production. Now, I should explain this term *pilot plant* before I go any farther. A chemist is a person who can work out a new process in the laboratory. And that is far from being the same thing as being able to operate it on a large scale. There are problems I don't have to go into now. But to develop a new process isn't the same thing as taking the process from the laboratory into commercial operation. This has to go through pilot plant, which is intermediate in size between the laboratory equipment and the big plant that you are going to build, if all goes well. And that pilot plant for nylon—and I've been through it—was at Deepwater, New Jersey. Now it may happen, if the chemistry is very similar to something you are already doing—once in a while, if you have everyone from the Board of Directors on down, and he likes to gamble, and he has a bit of courage—it may happen that you skip pilot plant, but never on anything brand new like this. They had never done anything like this before, and they found a lot of tricks on nylon 66, which was the first nylon. They found that if they took the diamine, which was basic, and the dicarboxylic acid, which of course was acidic, and put them together, they would form a salt. Now it's very important that you should have exactly equal molecular amounts of these two reagents, because if you have an excess of one or the other, the chain stops growing and the length of the chain isn't as long as it ought to be, and therefore the strength of the fiber isn't what it ought to be. So they found that if they put these together, and then let them crystalize, they would automatically adjust to a one-to-one basis, which you had to have. That was one of the tricks they found in pilot plants. They put it through the pilot plant, they made a silklike fiber, and they got it into commercial production just in time for World War II for the parachutes: If we hadn't had nylon for parachutes—we certainly didn't have silk from Japan for World War II—if we hadn't had nylon for parachutes, the death rate in the aviation group would have been twice, maybe three or four times what it was. And this was the first truly synthetic fiber. Now what do we have? We have a whole smear of them! And synthetic fibers in this country are larger in tonnage than our natural fibers. This all started, or let's say it continued, with the pilot plant in Deepwater, New Jersey, which is across the river from the experimental station of du Pont, which happens to be at Wilmington, Delaware.

The next story I want to talk about starts with the company we now call Exxon. Someone had had the idea for quite a while that, since we have a big chemical industry based on coal tar—I'm speaking now of the early 1920s—so should we have a big chemical industry based on petroleum. And now this has grown so far that coal tar is a relatively trivial source of organic chemicals in this country. And ninety percent of our synthetic organic chemicals are made from petroleum or natural gas; natural gas is simply the volatile end of petroleum. What was the first petrochemical, wouldn't you be interested to know? That was isopropyl alcohol, and that was started by a little company in New

Jersey, which Exxon, then Standard Oil of New Jersey, had bought out, and started making isopropyl alcohol. And that's where the enormous petrochemical industry, which is the biggest organic chemical industry, worldwide, that we have —that's where that began, right here in New Jersey. Now, before we leave the subject of petroleum, I want to tell you another story.

There was a French automobile driver by the name of Eugene Houdry. Mr. Houdry was not a chemist; he was a race-car driver. But he thought he could make the automobiles go faster on the race course if he had better gasoline. So he hired a chemist and said, "Find out how to make better gasoline." The chemist started working on it, and after a while he said, "I'm not only getting better gasoline, I'm getting more gasoline from a barrel of crude." So Mr. Houdry came over to this country—this is where the big petroleum companies are—and tried to interest them in this new idea. Of course, he went first to the big ones. He ran across what is called the NIH syndrome; in this case it doesn't stand for National Institutes of Health, but for Not Invented Here. The only thing that a chemical company can do when they have a new idea presented to them is to turn it over to the research department. The attitude of the research department, inevitably, human nature being what it is, is this. *We* were supposed to have made these fine discoveries; if this one is any good, why, we're going to look bad, so let's find some way of knocking it down. They will never say that, but that's at the back of their mind, and don't you forget it! So he went to number 1, number 2, number 3, number 4, number 5, number 6, number 7, to number 8. The first seven said "no good"; number 8 happened to be Sun Oil Company. I happen to be an old friend of the man who was Research Director of it at that time, Mr. Pugh, who said, "Jack Bruun, you find out if this man has any-

thing." After six weeks, Jack went back to Mr. Pugh and said,
"I'm almost sure he has something very good." Mr. Pugh
said, "Jack, 'almost' isn't good enough. I'm not going to build
a plant on 'almost.' When you're absolutely sure, then come
back and tell me." Well, they stopped everything else in the
research laboratory and went to work on it, and then Jack
Bruun came back to Mr. Pugh and said, "He's got something!" So they built a plant.

This happened just before World War II, when we were
going to need a lot of high octane gasoline, both for automobiles and for aviation. Of course, after Sun Oil made a
great success of it, Exxon wanted to get in too. They didn't
want their competitors to have a better process than they
had, so they said, "Alright, how much is it going to cost us?"
Mr. Houdry was a little bit greedy and said, "Fifty million
bucks." Back in the 1930s that was a lot of dough! And so
Mr. Murphree of Exxon called his group together with the
aid of my old company, Kellogg, and said, "There has to be
some better way of doing this that will avoid Mr. Houdry's
patents." And they found it; it's called fluidized bed cracking, and at the present time, about ninety-five percent of the
cracking that's done in the world is done by this fluidized
bed. I'm not going to tell you the details of it, because you'd
forget it anyhow, but if you want to find out about fluidized
bed cracking, all you have to do is go to the Kirk Othmer
Encyclopedia of Chemical Technology, which I'm sure is in
the Library, and read about it. It's a fascinating way of doing
things, and that happened right here in New Jersey, by the
collaboration of M. W. Kellogg and Exxon.

As so often happens, there is a sequel to this story. When
I was head of the Department at Purdue, there was a very
smart young graduate, again a son of a missionary, by the
name of C. J. Plank, who went to work for Mobil. A little
over a year ago, I gave Dr. Plank the Chemical Pioneer

Award of the American Institute of Chemists, because he had found a far better catalyst than Mr. Houdry ever found or than Exxon ever found. Why is it better? Two things. It makes the reaction go one hundred times as fast. One hundred times as fast—this is quite exceptional; and instead of getting about fifty-two percent of gasoline, you get about eighty-two percent of gasoline—and I told you I wouldn't talk about anything this evening except what had multi-billion-dollar implications and I will tell you how much this saves the United States every year. In crude oil, we do not have to buy from the OPEK countries or from anyone else. Two billion bucks' worth of crude oil every year is saved by C. J. Plank's catalyst, and that happened right here in the state of New Jersey.

The last incident has to do with my old company. I didn't have anything personally to do with this, so I'm not bragging about anything I did. But before I was with Kellogg, a man by the name of Henry McGrath ran across the fact that metallurgists had proluced alloys that can be operated at higher temperatures, and without softening too much, than the alloys that were available up to that time. Now, what does that have to do with synthesizing ammonia? Well, the way you get the hydrogen to make ammonia is by making steam react with natural gas. Natural gas is mostly methane; methane has the formula CH_4, and if you have had any chemistry at all, you can visualize this equation: H_2O, hot steam, CH_4 methane gives CO, carbon monoxide and $_3H_2$'s, 3 molecules of hydrogen, but you have to put a double arrow in there, because that reaction goes forward or backward, and that's the trouble with it. As you raise the temperature, the reaction goes forward better, which is what you want; when you raise the pressure, it pushes the reaction backward, which you don't want. But now, because we could use a higher temperature than we could ever use before, because of what the metallurgists had done, maybe we could also stand using a higher pressure—which is undesirable from the standpoint of driving the reaction to completion, but is very desirable from the standpoint of how big the compressor has to be. If you add up one molecule of gas, CH_4, on the left of this equation, there's CO plus $3H_2$4 molecules on the right of the equation, so the more the compression on the natural gas, the more you save on your compressor. And that ain't hay! Because you can save so much on your compressor, you can throw away a whole floor of reciprocating compressors, which are very expensive to install and to maintain. You have to put enormous foundations under them, because as this heavy piston goes back and forth, there's vibration, inevitably, and if you don't put a lot of reinforced concrete under them, then they shake themselves apart after awhile. Instead of that, you put in a rotary compressor, which is almost vibrationless. So that's one place you can save because of this discovery of my friend Henry McGrath. You can also save by putting in a secondary reformer, it's called, in which you take this very hot gas, which has been mostly converted over to CO and hydrogen, and you mix very hot air. With that the temperature goes crazy of course, because some of the natural gas burns in the air you have introduced, and in this secondary reformer, the temperature goes so hot that no cheap, strong material could stand it. So what you have is a steel shell, with aluminum insulation on the inside, that keeps the heat from getting to the steel, and then you can contain this very ferocious condition. That means the methane practically disappears, and you have introduced the nitrogen that is necessary for the ammonia synthesis, without liquefying air. So now we have our hydrogen and our nitrogen—though there's a little cleanup that has to come in here that we won't spend any time on—then we compress them; and the next equation, the last one I'll bother you with, is $N_2 + 3H_2$ gives $2NH_3$, again with double arrow showing that it goes backward and forward. This is how you make ammonia. Well, why is ammonia so important? People think of ammonia as something you have in a household detergent that smells pretty strong; actually eighty percent of the ammonia is used to make fertilizer. Forty percent of all the fertilizer made in the world is made from ammonia, and the arithmetic comes out this way: one pound of plant food, properly distributed, will give you ten pounds of extra grain or anything else you want to raise. So at the present time, the net result of these improvements I've been discussing with you is that the cost of making ammonia was cut in half and, as a result of that, half of the ammonia capacity of the entire world has been made by Kellogg. Kellogg has ammonia plants operating on every continent except one, I wonder if anyone can guess which continent doen't have any? Antarctica, right! All the other continents have Kellogg ammonia plants, and that gives us enough fertilizer to produce enough extra food to feed three hundred million people!

DR. CITRON: Thank you, Dr. Hass. I'm sure that you will all agree that already the level of New Jersey has risen by two thousand feet above sea level. We can begin to see that, small a state though we are in area, we have made a distinct contribution to chemistry, and perhaps to many other fields if we look into it a little more deeply. Our second speaker, who is filling in for Dr. Pollara of Stevens Institute, is a well-known chemist in his own right. Dr. A. K. Bose earned his Sc.D. degree at Massachusetts Institute of Technology; he did postdoctoral work, if I'm not mistaken, at Harvard University with Dr. Woodward, who is a Nobel Prize winner; and he has been a professor of chemistry at Stevens Institute since 1959. Prior to 1959 he was a research chemist with the Upjohn Company, in Michigan. He has done significant research in synthetic organic chemistry, and he has written one book on the synthesis of penicillin and one on the synthesis of beta-lactams. For his research at Stevens Institute he has received over three hundred thousand dollars worth of grants from the National Institute of Health, and anyone who has tried to get a grant will know how significant that is. He is a recipient of the Otten's award for excellence in research at Stevens Institute, he is a Fellow of the New York Academy of Sciences, and he has written no less than one hundred forty publications. I think that you will all have a distinct pleasure, as I will, in listening to Dr. A. K. Bose from Stevens Institute of Technology.

B. A. K. Bose

DR. BOSE: Dr. Citron, ladies and gentlemen, this is an unexpected pleasure, because until this afternoon I did not know that I would have the opportunity of visiting this beautiful campus and also to meet some of our own alumni, Art Conway and Art Murphy, and have the opportunity of following such an eminent speaker as Dr. Hass.

Dr. Hass has talked to you about catalysts, about "reforming." I will talk about the same things but in a different context. When I talk about a catalyst, it will have to do with "raw" students, and teachers trying to get them excited about chemistry, so that in time they will create new things, new processes, new drugs, or new equations that would contribute to human knowledge and to a betterment of the standard of living. When I talk about "reforming," it will be with reference to the mode of teaching, the way you get a student to have more faith in himself, and the way you persuade him to put forward that extra effort that must go with the touch of genius.

New Jersey is a small state but it has a very large number of people. As a matter of fact, Hoboken, which is the city where Stevens Institute is located and where I have spent many years, is sandwiched between two tunnels, the Lincoln tunnel and the Holland tunnel. It is about a square mile in area, and it has about 55,000 people. To tell you the truth, I do not miss the crowds of Calcutta when I go into Hoboken.

New Jersey is a special state because of this tremendous density of population and the diversity of chemical industry that Dr. Hass has spoken of. If an atom bomb were to be dropped on New Jersey, the people in the rest of the country would die from lack of medicine because seventy percent of the drugs produced in the United States either are manufactured in New Jersey or the research and development work related to them are carried out in New Jersey. I can recite a long list of names of drug companies such as Merck, Squibb, Schering, Warner Lambert, Sandoz, Ciba-Geigy, Roche, and the like that are located in New Jersey. Chemical companies related to the petrochemical industries have been mentioned earlier by Dr. Hass. We should not forget Allied Chemicals, which is involved in almost every kind of business you can think of, including raising of catfish (perhaps you did not know about that one!) .

Since all these different kinds of industry are heavily reliant on chemistry and since we have this large population here, you would expect that New Jersey is producing a very large number of chemists. But that is not so.

With the special power that Deans and Provosts have, Professor Pollara was able to summon, in a day or two, a great deal of statistics, which he gave to me. I am told that in the state of New Jersey there are roughly a little less than five hundred undergraduates at any time who claim to major in chemistry, and about the same number of graduate students who show a great love for chemistry. Now that is a little bit unusual, this rough equality in the number of undergraduates and graduates, but apart from that, the numbers in themselves are rather small compared to the population, or to the importance of chemistry to the state. If you count the number of chemistry faculty at FDU at your three campuses, Seton Hall, Princeton, Stevens, and a few other colleges that are involved in research, the number barely comes to one hundred. I am talking about the completely academically oriented people and genuine chemists.

How does that compare with the rest of the country? It seems that there are some twelve thousand academic-type chemists, either as regular faculty members of universities or as residents on campuses who spend most of their time in research related to chemistry. So, the number of academic research chemists in New Jersey is of the size of the statistical error in counting the total number in the country—less than one hundred out of twelve thousand!

I am glad to say, however, that the significance of the contribution made by this rather small number of chemists is far out of proportion to their percentage. Fortunately, these chemists have made quite a few inventions that are very important and they have also added to the basic knowledge that is needed to make a better world for all of us. I would like to name a few of these. If you have been around for a long time you would know that Princeton has always been highly regarded by physical chemists. (I myself, am an organic chemist, so I cannot speak with any great fervor about physical chemistry). Professor Hugh Taylor, who became Sir Hugh, was an Englishman who was knighted by the Queen of England and, it turns out, also by the Pope. He established a tremendous reputation for the school of physical chemistry at Princeton, and chemists from not only the other states of the Union, but also all over the world tried to have the opportunity to spend some time at Princeton in the physical chemistry group. Over a long period of time, Sir Hugh and his associates contributed to the area of physical chemistry; much of it related to catalysis. As you heard from Dr. Hass, catalysis has been an extremely important ingredient for the success of the petrochemical industry. And this has played a very important role in the life of this country. During World War II it was very important to have enough energy, especially fuel in the liquid form, to be able to transport men and materials, and to be able to carry out the production of different types of industrial chemicals. So the science of catalysis proved extremely important for the very survival of the nation. New Jersey has certainly contributed handsomely in the academic as well as industrial aspects of catalysis.

There have been other areas of chemistry that have all of a sudden come into prominence. For example, before 1943, I doubt whether too many chemists from the rest of the world and, for that matter, from the other states of the Union, were much aware of Rutgers University as a place where important contributions would be made in chemistry or associated sciences. But in 1943 Professor Selman Waksman presented to the world the fruits of his labor in the field of microbiology, which is closely tied to chemistry. He came up with a powerful antibiotic; he even coined the word *antibiotic*. He discovered streptomycin, which has saved hundreds of thousands of lives all over the world. This is one of the most powerful weapons to fight tuberculosis.

Some of you may know that a long time ago, even before most of you were born, the Catskills had become very important for the health of the Eastern part of the United

States. At that time thousands contracted tuberculosis every year and the only thing that the doctors could prescribe for them was nutritious food, sunshine, and a reasonable amount of good cheer and happiness. These things they got by going to the Catskills. There was plenty of good food that some of those bountiful widows cooked, and there was lots of sunshine and nice scenery and interesting things to do in the Catskills. But do you know that all those places had to be closed down recently? Even the first-rate nursing homes for tubercular patients have disappeared. There is no need for them anymore because of the success of the anti-tubercular medicines, the foremost of which is streptomycin, discovered by Waksman. Since 1943 many chemists, micro-biologists, and others who deal with different areas of organic chemistry, biochemistry, and medicinal chemistry, have made their pilgrimage to Rutgers, to what is now the Waksman Research Institute, to learn about new ways of combating different types of infection.

A large portion of the time of an organic chemist is devoted to copying Mother Nature, who is very good at putting molecules together that are complex and have unusual properties. Organic chemists have to struggle with all sorts of special equipment and exotic chemicals when they try to duplicate the various molecules that are produced with such ease by the lowliest forms of life: by fungi, bacteria, sponges, and lichens. From this kind of research on biosynthesis many contributions to basic sciences have been made. Let me give you one example of an outstanding development from biosynthetic research conducted in a New Jersey drug company.

Years ago Dr. Carl Folkers at the Merck Research Institute was working on some problem of commercial interest that I am sure was intended to make a lot of money for the shareholders of Merck Company. However, in the course of this research, he came upon a very interesting small molecule that has been named *mevalonic acid*. It has six carbon atoms and is made out of nothing more exotic than the vinegar you use in Italian dressing for your salad. But this molecule loses one carbon atom, and the remaining five arrange themselves in a particular fashion (branched chain structure) ; this new molecule is the so-called isoprene unit, which seems to be a favorite building block for nature. Several different types of organic compounds, including steroids, are assembled in this fashion in living things. So the research of Folkers and his coworkers brought a much clearer understanding of the genesis of many compounds that are essential for life processes. For example, if the right kind of steroid hormone was not formed in the body, men would not have their "machismo" to brag about nor would women be as alluring as they would like to be.

Following the example of Dr. Hass, I might tell you a story or two—but nothing like the tale about his mythical brother Seymour! I am reminded of the time in the thirties when steroid sex hormone therapy was really something new, and estrone and testosterone were almost X-rated words. At that time those compounds had to be isolated from glands of animals, such the the gonads and the ovaries of cattle and pigs. There was this one laboratory in Switzerland that was devoted to isolating the female hormone estrone. In small amounts estrone can do wonders for women having various kinds of problems related to hormone imbalance. This company, believe it or not, had a terrible time. If they hired a man, and he worked there for any length of time, no matter how careful he was he would ingest some of the estrone through his skin or through his breathing, and pretty soon he would have a rounded appearance and his voice would be a little bit different. People would start making remarks. Since those were not liberated times, the poor fellow would have a problem; he would quit and go away to some distant place. So, the company would hire women, but no matter how plain she was to begin with, pretty soon she would have so much "s.a." that she would get married and quit.

Well, coming back to the more prosaic academic world I would like to tell you another story. This has to do with one of Stevens' contributions to chemistry in this country.

Many years ago a young instructor came to Stevens to teach, and as usual, the head of the department insisted that he teach so many freshman classes and so many sophomore classes, and be sure to give enough homework, grade all the papers, and so on—you know, the kind of thing that Dr. Citron has to do every morning and afternoon. Probably he was as harried as some of the younger faculty, like Art Murphy here. This poor fellow wanted to do some research; he seemed to have a knack for it. As a matter of fact, some big companies were willing to pay him cash to use him as a consultant and to have him do some research. But while he would be lecturing in one of the large lecture halls in the Morton building of Stevens, a little stink bomb would go off in one corner or a little fire would start with a piece of sodium thrown into a waste basket. He decided to give up teaching and go to one of the companies that was interested in his research. Fortunately, the company he joined was very generous; he was told that he could do any type of research he wanted as long as he himself was satisfied and his talents were being fully utilized. He confessed later in life that whenever his boss would come to his laboratory, he would feel sort of guilty because he was not trying to make money for his company. Some of you may have guessed that this was Irving Langmuir working at Schenectady for General Electric Company.

Dr. Langmuir became interested in such fundamental

things as molecules spreading themselves so thin that they form layers that are only one molecule thick. In course of time he discovered many properties of such monomolecular layers and contributed to our understanding of the interaction of molecules. His academic type of "pure" research paid handsome dividends for G.E. because, based on his research, it was possible to develop a great deal of practical technology for better lights, improved electric bulbs with long life, electric light of much higher intensity, and the like.

Dr. Langmuir continued with his basic research at G.E. and eventually received a Nobel Prize for his fundamental contributions. Stevens can take some credit for his prize, because he might not have thought of joining G.E. but for the classroom experience at Stevens! Langmuir was in a special category among American Nobel Prize winners—he was a native-born American. In those days it was not unusual for an American to get a Nobel Prize, but if you listened to his accent you would find in most cases that the Nobel Laureate had come from distant shores.

Nearly two decades ago when I came to New Jersey, I used to feel concerned about my accent when I went to some important pharmaceutical research conference. But I need not have worried since you had to look hard to find a group of native-born chemists at major conferences. That situation has changed greatly. Right now not too many scientists are coming from foreign lands. Today you would find it difficult to get a German or Dutch scientist to join your laboratory; they make more money in terms of dollars back in their own country because of the disparity between the value of the dollar and the value of the German mark or the Dutch guilder. In New Jersey you meet many chemists with a Southern drawl or the charming accents that you hear in some of the hills, or the special way of speaking they have on the West coast. The major universities that produce Ph.D.'s by the hundreds are in places like Wisconsin, California, Illinois. So the Ph.D.'s and other professional chemists who are manning the laboratories and doing industrial or basic research in New Jersey are mostly from outside the state. We do not mind that; the United States is one big country and one should be able to work in any part of it. But it may be instructive to examine more closely this migration of chemists to New Jersey. An obvious reason for this migration could be the lack of adequate numbers of properly trained chemists produced by New Jersey institutions.

To prepare oneself for creative work in chemistry, to learn chemistry in all its intricacies, to get a flavor of what it is all about, you have to do research. You could not just have a shelf full of books and get so excited reading them that you become a productive chemist in the true sense of the word. Most students must have something tangible to work with before reaching the creative stage; abstract ideas are not enough. If you are in the pharmaceutical industry, you will often hear that "you cannot feed an idea to a rat to test it; you have to have a compound to put inside a rat, and somebody has to make that compound." How true!

When you are planning research, you have to gather all kinds of chemicals and all kinds of instruments. In this connection there is a phenomenon that is particularly relevant to the research scene in the United States. Since World War II, whenever a physicist finds an application of an abstruse principle to the making of an exotic measurement, some industrial company decides that it is worthwhile to manufacture an instrument based on this new application. In due course, a "pushbutton" instrument package appears on the market with a price tag of ten thousand dollars or even one hundred thousand dollars on it. If you are an aggressive research scientist and have the right credentials, you write a stream of research proposals and sooner or later you get a grant from NIH or NSF to buy this new "toy."

Chemists usually treat these instrument packages as "black boxes." They may not know what is inside any more than many drivers know what is under the hood of a car. All that is really important is that the chemist should be able to introduce a chemical sample into one end of his "black box" and out of the other end should come a spectrum from which useful information can be gleaned. Hopefully, the mechanism inside would not break down too often and refuse to produce meaningful data.

It takes a great deal of money not only to buy these "black boxes" but to keep them in good operating condition. Heads of research departments and deans of science are usually delighted to buy these exotic "black boxes" that make such good conversation pieces, but they often forget to take into account the heavy expense of maintenance and operation. If you send for an engineer from the manufacturing company to repair one of these instruments, he charges two to three hundred dollars just to step inside your laboratory, and even if he fails to repair your instrument he sends you a bill. Doing modern research is a very expensive proposition! But research is still the best way of teaching a student chemistry and getting him all excited about his learning process.

It appears that you and I, who live in New Jersey and pay our taxes in New Jersey, do not like to spend very much of our tax money for higher education. Because if we did, we would not be listed close to Mississippi at the very bottom of the list of states, in terms of state funds for higher education—I do not mean just chemistry, but higher education in general. And since chemisty is a fairly expensive item, whatever is said about higher education in general applies with a great deal of truth to the teaching of chemistry. The question may be asked, what is wrong with producing a small number of chemists in New Jersey? Before I answer that, let me survey for you the recent fluctuations in technological manpower utilization in the United States.

A few years ago, when President Kennedy was in the White House, there was a major push to move the country forward in many technological directions. The Russian Sputnik had given us a kick in the pants, and intensive efforts were being made to attain excellence in all areas of science and technology. A huge space project was started to land a man on the moon; many lesser projects were undertaken by industry and academia. There were not enough scientists and engineers with adequate background to carry out all the projects on board. So what happened?

We got technical people from all over the world to come here. Scientists and engineers came from England, from Germany, and from many other countries, including even the "developing countries." But in a few years, when the space projects started folding up, the electronics industry was in trouble, and there was a downturn in the economy, research laboratories started to lay off technical staff. Many industrial companies seem to have the policy, when profits are good and there is quite a bit of money around, of starting research and hiring technical staff and then, as soon as the profit figures look unpromising, firing the research people first. If in a few years the pendulum swings in the other direction, they start research again and vie with other companies for the available technical people.

This "on again-off again" research situation is very harmful in the long run. Right now many of the technical people from abroad have returned to their own countries but, more important, the native sons have decided to keep away from the hard and poverty-stricken life in graduate school. So, if the economy turns around in two or three years, there will be a shortage of highly trained young Americans. This time there will be a problem in getting trained people from other countries. The technically advanced countries of Europe will no longer be good recruiting ground as in the past. The developing countries will strenuously oppose "brain-drain" and will place engineers and scientists who are trying to emigrate. Therefore, the best policy for America seems to be to get the native-born interested in higher education and technical training. But how to motivate him? Whether we like it or not, a job with a good salary is the strongest incentive for most students to pursue higher studies. So at present we have to discover other ways of stimulating the interest of the potential graduate student.

The stability in the graduate student population in universities is very important because science or chemistry is not something that you can put on the shelf and take off the shelf as you need it. Science cannot go in spurts; there has to be a continuity. You cannot all of a sudden start expanding a laboratory, or contracting it, without doing a great deal of harm. Now, many of us do not realize that three to five years may be a very small period—a small quantum of time in the life of a nation, or the life of a university, but it is a pretty big slice of the creative period in the life of a chemist or a scientist; if somebody has missed that particular quantum, he may never be able to make up for that again.

I am sorry to say that in the last few years a whole generation of potential graduate students has been skipped. Universities all across the land have had to be content with the diminishing size of the graduate school. A few universities in New York even had to discontinue the Ph.D. program in certain fields, including chemistry, because the number of students in the program was below the critical limit for a meaningful research and scholarly atmosphere. This is a spiraling situation—the fewer the research students the smaller is the chance of research funds and the possibility of continued research. How to sustain research under the prevailing conditions and how to keep the research atmosphere alive are problems that many of the smaller universities face much more acutely than the major institutions.

I have given a great deal of thought to this problem in the context of the colleges and universities in New Jersey. There is at least a partial solution that I have been able to find. As a teacher of many years' standing I have worked closely with students—many of them undergraduates. I can assure you that we have untapped resources with which to enhance the research capability of chemistry departments in New Jersey. Among our undergraduates we have our share of bright minds, inquisitive minds. But many of these students do not know their research potential. Maybe they come from a home where nobody has been close to science. Give such students a sense of excitement, a bit of challenge, and, most of all, the opportunity to discover their own potential for creativity in science, and watch for the gratifying results. I have done this at Stevens and have been amazed at the amount of talent that can be saved for the good of the individual as well as the country.

Many of you parents and teachers must have noted that in the sixties the young college students started to yearn for a sense of relevancy. They wanted their studies and their lives to be relevant, and they wanted to do something for society and for humanity. The science-oriented students discovered the field of medicine as a near-perfect solution for their urge for relevancy, and on every campus science and engineering students started a swing toward "premed" programs. Organic chemistry, biology, and biochemistry courses swelled in size with such rapidity that there was consternation among deans and the faculty of physics and mathematics!

The cynic pointed out that by becoming an M.D. one not only became highly relevant to society and served humanity but also had a good possibility of sixty to seventy thousand dollars or more per year in earning, a huge house in a suburb, and even a beautiful socialite as a wife. The cynic made the valid prediction that, with nearly everyone trying to enter medical school, there would be cutthroat competition and only a quarter of those trying would be able to enter any medical school in this country or even abroad.

This setting gave me an opportunity for trying an experiment with undergraduates to discover hidden talent for research. Having lived long in this country, I knew that to get funds from the deans and the president I would need a catchy name for what I wanted to do. So I coined the acronym UPTAM—nothing to do with upward mobility really, but this name proved adequate for the purpose. I did get the funds I wanted from the president of Stevens! UPTAM actually stands for *U*ndergraduate *P*rojects in *T*echnology *a*nd *M*edicine. This program provides summer support to carefully selected undergraduates to participate in research in the biomedical area under the joint supervision of a medical school faculty member and a Stevens faculty member. The intent here is to apply the science/engineering background of Stevens students to some real problem in the field of medicine. To qualify for this program an undergraduate has to have a genuine interest in medicine or related biomedical research or the broad field of life sciences; the student must also have shown, in one way or another, some special talent or intellectual inquisitiveness. The UPTAM participants then choose programs of interest to them individually from a number of alternatives available. It is a distinct personal pleasure for me to be able to report that over a period of five years this program has been very successful and it has contributed in a very tangible fashion to the quantity as well as quality of research at Stevens.

Before describing the UPTAM program further I would

like to tell you one of the stories heard in medical circles. They say that if you went to a small medical center, say in Nebraska, you would find an M.S. in the front room running computers and auto-analyzers while the M.D. is sitting in the back room counting money. This may be an overstatement, but not by much.

The field of medicine has so much input available from science and engineering that no average M.D. could cope with the situation by himself. Modern medicine has to be a team effort because of the high level of science and engineering infusion that is handled best by experts who need not be M.D.'s. One ingredient of the success of the UPTAM program has been the intellectual caliber of the Stevens students and the background of science/engineering that they bring to bear on the medical problem they are studying. One chemical engineering undergraduate, Jerry Granato '75, designed an "iron lung" made of space-age plastic. This was a jacketlike device that allowed the patient to sit up and have a great deal of freedom of movement while receiving aid to respiration. With this research experience to his credit, Jerry received admission to the Johns Hopkins School of Medicine. Another student, Martha Connolly '75, has also gone to Johns Hopkins but is studying biomedical engineering there; she had synthesized difficult-to-obtain isomers of sterols by a new synthetic method. Other students have made worthwhile contributions working on projects such as "diagnostic tests for acute pancreatitis," "diffusion coefficients of packed red blood cells," "biochemical characteristics of a cancer," and "lipid changes in shock." Many of the UPTAM students got so devoted to research that they continued with their summer project through the academic year. This type of research led to several undergraduate theses for additional academic recognition. Some UPTAM participants have become coauthors of papers in internationally known journals, and some have presented their research findings at professional meetings.

The research effort by bright undergraduates—often as teammates for advanced students such as senior Ph.D. students or postdoctorals—has raised the general level of research performance in our department. The students have discovered that the UPTAM research experience can brighten their employment picture very substantially. One UPTAM student, Judy Jamieson '76, who investigated a new approach to cholesterol analysis, is now a junior chemist at Merck with a handsome salary. She was selected in competition with graduates from several major universities. I could give many more examples but will content myself with only one more illustration of undergraduate interest in research. The youngest UPTAM participant has been Darla Latawiec '80, who started her project during the summer even before she became a freshman at Stevens.

The UPTAM program has clearly demonstrated that if interesting, challenging, and timely programs are devised, it is easy to motivate undergraduates to participate in meaningful research. And, if they can be teamed with advanced research workers, valuable contributions can be expected from them. In support of this proposition I can cite from our own experience with research in the penicillin field. Some ten years ago we devised a new total synthesis of penicillin and analogs that is now widely used by pharmaceutical research laboratories to create new potential antibiotics. The projects on penicillin research in our laboratory have always attracted bright undergraduates; working closely with postdoctorals (several undergraduates to one postdoctoral) on the project, they have added significantly to our recent contributions to this field. In turn these undergraduates have been able to obtain fellowships at major graduate schools largely on the basis of their demonstrated research ability.

In short, if the setting is right in terms of interesting research topics and advanced research students to work with, there can be an enhancement factor: the undergraduate effort gets raised to a much higher level of performance and achievement.

So now you have my plan for making New Jersey play a much more important role in chemical research than the small number of graduate students and faculty may seem to warrant at first sight. We have college campuses with adequate capacity, we have industrial foundations and private benefactors who care about chemistry, and even the state government is now becoming sensitive to the needs of higher education. Most important of all, we have a large number of bright undergraduates who are growing up in an atmosphere of chemistry in this state. After all, the Garden State is not really much of a garden; calling it the "Chemical State" would not be wrong. We inhale many chemicals but we are also intellectually much more aware of chemistry all around us than the residents of most other states. Our promising undergraduates are thus quite susceptible to the allure of a research career in chemistry.

If the pharmaceutical and chemical industries and the universities and the educationists in the state coordinate their effort, we can discover the latent chemists early and entice them into the field of research. In time this will catalyze the blossoming of chemical talent in the state that will contribute to the betterment of the world around us.

DR. CITRON: I'd just like to make a brief comment about Dr. Bose's remark. Stevens Institute and Fairleigh Dickinson University have always seemed to cooperate hand in hand, as far as chemistry is concerned, and we have a number of students who went on from our undergraduate program into Stevens Institute to take up chemistry at the higher levels and to earn their Ph.D.'s, and they now are teaching again in our own institution: Dr. Murphy, Dr. Starrick, Dr. Kevra on a part-time basis, and Dr. Hoffman, Dr. Krychuk, and, on occasion, Dr. Lepore (he's almost a Ph.D.), and I must say that is an enviable record. We seem to find that the home-grown product here in New Jersey is, after all, the best. Time and again we have gone back to our own product, our own home-grown product, rather than to more fruitful fields, to higher institutions of learning. They have come back to us to show us we can educate chemists, first-rate chemists, and I am sure these people will be first-rate chemists in the future, wherever they may be. I am sure we will be proud they came from New Jersey, and I am sure many other institutions can say the same thing.

DR. ANGOFF: In my ignorance, I always thought it was Germany that led the world in chemistry, and I am very happy to learn today that it is Passaic, and Clifton, and New Jersey. But seriously, how do we compare with the other countries?

DR. HASS: May I comment on that? Recently the editor of one of the journals of the American Chemical Society gave me a remarkable assignment. He asked me to go through the sixty-four years of publications of industrial and engineering chemistry—and for most of those years, there were two thousand, six hundred pages a year of printed matter—and select the twelve most important articles that had ever been published in that journal. Well, that took some doing. I read pretty fast and I was familiar with a lot of what was published in the journal. I did the job last summer, and these twelve articles are now being reprinted, one each month in *Chemical Technology*. In going through these journals I found some interesting statistics, and one of them is this: how do you suppose the dollar value of the import of chemicals from Germany to the United States in 1913 compared to the dollar value of the exports of chemicals from the United States to Germany in 1913? Anyone want to guess on that one?

A.:   Bigger than the United States.

DR. HASS: You'd heard this before! We sent them one hundred fifty-six million dollars worth and they sent us sixty million dollars worth in 1913, and most people will tell you we didn't even have a chemical industry in 1913 in the United States. We had the biggest chemical industry in the world in 1913 here in the United States, and don't let anyone tell you differently!

How is it now?

Now it's much bigger than anybody else's; there just isn't any comparison. Now, another way of looking at it would be: Where have the Nobel Prizes gone in the last twenty-five years? Well, the United States has far more than anyone else. All my grandparents came from Germany. I'm not prejudiced against Germans in any way, and they have some great chemists—but they don't have as many great chemists as we have, no one has as many great chemists as we have.

DR. BOSE: Dr. Hass, you will agree with me that if you open up any of the major journals of today, journals of the American Chemical Society, the Chemcom from England, any journal, you will find the contributions coming out of two countries from outside, Germany and Japan. There is a sustained level in the case of Japan, that is gradually going up, both in quantity and, more important, in quality, whereas in America we started out with a very large base and are still holding our own, but a lot of people who know this area from both the industrial and the academic side have started wondering how long we can patch up and manage if there isn't a real effort made. It was very encouraging to read in the newspaper a few months ago, of President Ford's quoting parts of a report by the National Science Foundation that mentioned some of these statistics, and saying that the country should not be allowed to take things on and off the shelves as far as science and research were concerned. However, we have to remember that the election isn't very far away, and after November what will really be done is something else again, unless enlightened people take a positive action and a society such as the American Chemical Society promulgate a specific philosophy to pursue. We should not be too sure that, just because in the past we have done so well, we'll continue to do so in the future. There's a good potential for it, but you always have to watch when you are Number One. You are always going to find an Avis around the corner.

Q.: You were so inspiring with the suggestion that American students develop their potential in various interesting areas, and I am intrigued by a friend of mine who has three adopted children. They are very well fixed financially, and the children are very bright students. The oldest boy would very much like to be a doctor, and they have had an absolutely dreadful time trying to get that boy into medical school. Our hospitals are filled with interns and doctors coming from all sections of the world, and we discover that this very, very interesting boy, a highly intelligent student, cannot find a place to go in any medical school in this country, the European countries will not accept an American student. The only way this very brilliant boy has been able to go to medical school is to the tune of thirty thousand dollars to get him in! What has happened to our American students that are not in a reciprocal situation with students in other places in the world, as far as we are concerned?

DR. BOSE: Let me tell you a little bit more of the sad story that you started to tell. When this very bright student finishes his studies, he'll have problems there because of the language, but when he gets over all these hurdles, finishes his studies, and he comes back home, the local medical societies will do everything possible to keep him away from their rosters. He'll have many tests to take. If he wants to practice in New Jersey, he'll have to take a set of tests, but if he decides next year to go to Florida, they'll insist he take another set of tests, because what they learn abroad is nothing, they say.

Q.: What about our American boys?

DR. BOSE: Those who have graduated from medical schools in this country don't have to take this set of tests. I've been told by the deans of medical schools that it almost ends up as a lottery, because roughly one out of four applications—highly qualified applications in a particular school—can be taken, and those top four are so close to each other that it's the predilection of the dean, or a whim, or an accident that removes one, two, and three, out of the four. How are you going to change this?

Q.: You cannot be an American student; you have to be from some other area.

DR. BOSE: No, those are coming from outside ready-made, and that's where those countries are screaming, because thousands and thousands of dollars are spent of their money and their limited resources to train those people, and they are coming, after their training, to America and staying here, because the facilities they are getting, apart from the money, are really very substantial. I have a younger brother who is a surgeon, so I can tell you from practical experience that the situation is what I'm saying. So it is not that the foreign students are coming and taking away the seeds from the American universities, for there are very few foreign students in American medical schools. The number of American medical boys and girls who would like to go to medical schools is about three to four times the capacities of the medical schools. There are different ways of changing this situation; they will take time, they will take money, and they will take a genuine effort, and some of us suspect that it will take at least an aquiescence on the part of the American Medical Association.

Q.:   One of the problems that we seem to face is that, after the young students graduate from college, after those six or seven long years of work, they find that the remuneration monetarily is much less than, say, having worked in business or some other field of endeavor, like being a bus driver, or a policeman or fireman in New York City. Sometimes the starting pay after six or seven years of hard labor is so low that he would have been better off at the age of nineteen to take the fireman's exam in New York City. I find that this tremendous disparity in salary remuneration is a defeating element in trying to make students chemists. I know that this is a fact, and what does Dr. Bose, being a chemist, think that we, as a group of teachers, could do, to remedy this, if anything?

DR. BOSE: This is the centennial of the American Chemical Society, just as it is the Bicentennial of the country, so the American Chemical Society, through its various organizations, has been trying to put before the public what they consider to be the more true image of the chemists. He is not the guy who put smokestacks in the sky and put carcinogens in your food, and so on, but he is the fellow who invents all sorts of new chemicals, new processes, new catalysts, etcetera. So the public relations job, in the better sense of the term, is very important. It is also very important to realize what the most successful new industries are. The most successful in America have the newer technology, because, let's face it, the strength of this country is in her technology. There are no two ways about it, the population is not something to brag about; the natural resources was something to brag about at one time, but not anymore. We have to make all sorts of compromises with little countries, because we want their copper, or we want their zinc, or we don't want to get cut off from their hydrocarbons, and so forth. The real strength America has is its technological superiority. We start out with a very high level of technological base; the lowest performance at the technical level in America is much higher than the average level of performance in Russia, for example. In Russia they can send Sputniks and space craft, but they have to buy razor blades from India. That gives you an understanding of how balanced their technology is. So, let's not forget for a single moment that America has to depend on technology, and chemistry, of course, as a major part of technology; and technologists, not to wither away, have to have the right kind of compensation. So it's a problem of such magnitude that public relations, better understanding, airing of the problem, and activity by the society, the American Chemical Society and other professional societies offer the only safeguard one can think of, the only practical safeguard.

DR. ANGOFF: It's very difficult to measure things with money. Barbara Walters probably gets more every year than most of the faculties of Harvard put together, but I'd rather not be Barbara Walters, for all kinds of reasons. But there is one thing I would like to say. I was brought up in the tradition—I come from Manhattan and Boston—that New Jersey, well . . . had mosquitoes, swamps, and not much else, but actually I learned today that if you took New Jersey away from the United States, the United States would be in very, very bad shape. So I wonder, why has the state of New Jersey been so poor in its public relations? I give you this idea free. Any suggestions?

MEMBER OF AUDIENCE: Dr. Angoff, I am interested in this question. I'm a former associate of Dr. Bose's, I was assistant director of research at Stevens, I retired from industry, and became an assistant director of research at Stevens Tech, and that is how I really got to know Dr. Bose. I think the question of employment of chemists, and for chemists, is of tremendous concern and is one that requires innovation and flexibility, and support surely, also. But chemists have been very rigid. Many of the highly trained chemists were trained to do doctoral theses, and many of them thought, "Well, this is my field. I will not get out of it, you can't get me out of this. I'm in this box and I'm going to stay there," and they wouldn't dirty their hands, some of these chemists. Now this is changing; there are fine chemists such as Dr. Hass, who dirtied his hands and got out into industry after being highly involved in research at Purdue. I think this shows that it is important for the chemist to keep an eye on where he can contribute and how he can contribute, not that he has to straitjacket himself and do only the same thing that he did in college. I've got interested in the field of employment. I'm on the national membership affairs committee and on the employment aids committee, and spent some time a year ago giving a paper on the subject of changing jobs.

And I think that chemists need to think about this. How do you keep a job? When do you change a job? This important question is one that I believe should occupy the chemist and is occupying the chemist.

DR. ANGOFF: Dr. Kron, do you want to come down here?

DR. KRON: I've been to many Leverton Lectures, and this is the first time I've given myself the privilege of speaking at one. Two items I'd like to give. One is in response to a previous question or comment about being sure that something is being done in the United States, not only to maintain, but to elevate the standards and also the quantity of our products so that we will continue to grow throughout the world. Some friends and I, acting as a program committee of the International Executives Association, put together a program and carried it out at a conference two weeks ago at the Waldorf, on the subject of the realities of foreign trade. What we did—our program for that conference—was to find out from the American international traders what it was that it was necessary for the United States government to do, first in the way of correcting laws we have governing international trade that are not working, second, of creating new laws needed to help international traders expand the trade of goods throughout the world, and third, of carrying out and executing treaties with other countries throughout the world, because, as you realize, we can't make laws in this country that will govern other countries. The idea of this conference was to gather all this material together and hear the actual requirements of the international profession, and put that into an authoritative document that the International Executive Association will bring down to Washington and put before people like the Secretary of Commerce and various committees of the Congress, and in that way put pressure on these people to help the international trader in his effort to produce and sell more goods abroad. Now, what that means is everything that's been talked about here—about additional opportunities for people, about having places where highly trained and highly educated technologists can work and produce—and we had as our stimulus the statistic, which has been proved, that the international field in the last ten years has produced an increase in the American work force, including technologists, of nineteen percent, whereas the strictly domestic companies of the United States produced an increase in the work force of only fourteen percent. So you see, if we have any success at all in this effort that we design and that we are going to carry out—as a matter of fact it's in the middle of being carried out—there will be many more opportunities for American boys and girls, technologists, and workers of every kind to share in the expansion of the sale of American goods abroad.

My second point is one that as a trustee of Fairleigh Dickinson University I just cannot let go by. One of the greatest attributes of the state of New Jersey is the fact that it houses the ninth largest private university in the United States—the largest university in the state, an outstanding school by the name of Fairleigh Dickinson University.

DR. ANGOFF: Any more questions? Again, thanks very much to the two speakers for giving us two superb talks. I really think that this was a historic evening in the history of the Leverton Lectures, and I repeat that they will appear in book form very soon. Thank you very much.